WHY KINGDOMS FALL

THE JOURNEY FROM BREAKDOWN TO RESTORATION

Bishop Paul S. Morton

Why Kingdoms Fall

THE JOURNEY FROM BREAKDOWN TO RESTORATION

Bishop Paul S. Morton

Albury Publishing
Tulsa, Oklahoma

4th Printing

Why Kingdoms Fall
The Journey From Breakdown to Restoration
ISBN 1-57778-078-7

Greater St. Stephen Full Gospel Baptist Church
9661 Lake Forest Boulevard
New Orleans, Louisiana 70127

Published by ALBURY PUBLISHING
P. O. Box 470406
Tulsa, Oklahoma 74147-0406

CONTENTS

ACKNOWLEDGMENTS

I first want to thank God for being with me and allowing me to go through this unique experience. I know I have become a vessel who is better equipped for His use in these last days. Through this experience I am able to write this book to increase the body of Christ.

Of course, I want to thank my wife, Debra, who has been there for me through the whole ordeal. She was the first person with whom I shared what God had revealed to me. She clearly understood my experience, but also helped me with some of the practical things in writing this book. I know it was intense. I love you.

I want to acknowledge the strength and support of my children, Paul, Jasmine, and Christiann. Dad appreciates your spiritual maturity. I am very proud that you are my children. Thanks to Christy for her vision of my new look and P. J. for the song, "I Resign." Also, love to Jasmine, my oldest, who stood right by my side.

To my brother and sisters, nieces and nephews, I really thank you for being my family. With your continued prayers and support, we will continue to break generational curses. I will always need you and love you very much.

Greater St. Stephen, I could never repay you for standing strong and being the kind of church that any pastor would love to shepherd. In spite of the pressure, you continued to stand. Your love, prayers, and kindness shown to me and my wife as co-pastor during this difficult time will never be forgotten. Thank you for being people who operate in "spirit over mind." I dedicate this book to you.

Special thanks to Elder Lester Love, my personal assistant, and Brother Patrick Johnson, Chief of Security, for your love, patience, and endurance. May God continue to bless you both.

God always surrounds you with those whom you need. I am speaking especially of Dr. Suzette Cullins. Dr. Cullins, thank you for being a spiritual woman as well as an excellent physician. My wife and I thank you. God has great things in store for you. To Drs. John and Arlene Barnett, my friends as well as my brother and sister in the Lord, thanks for fighting with me and for me in the Spirit. Debra and I adore you and cherish your friendship. Also, my appreciation goes to Dr. James Davis, my neighbor and personal physician, who made an old-fashioned house call. In the midst of your own personal matters, you took time out to care. May the Lord God strengthen you and keep you and bless you in all your endeavors. Special thanks to Dr. Anison, who shared with me the knowledge and experiences that brought clarity and comfort.

Thanks to Sister Bell Fabor for your skillful typing and commitment to excellence in spiritual things. Also, to Sister Floretta Grant, my sister Gwen, and my nephew Bobbie, for your brilliant writing abilities and your much needed help in getting this book together.

Finally, to my Full Gospel Baptist family, you are loved. Thanks for operating in the "full" Gospel, praying in the Spirit for me, and mightily doing spiritual warfare. By this, I was able to pull down the strongholds. I believe God allowed us to go through this type of warfare to prepare us for what lies ahead. We have been called to change a generation, and in doing so we must do serious spiritual warfare. It was necessary that we fight and see the manifestation in the earth realm. Praise God, we won the battle!

I especially want to thank the Bishops' Council for being there for me. I love you. Special thanks to Bishop Long for taking care of many details concerning my health. Thanks to Bishops Floyd, Long, Brister, Malone,

Ulmer, Wiley, McClendon, Morton, and Trotter for coming to see about me. Your fellowship and prayers kept me. You are special and have been chosen and called by God to an end-time purpose.

FOREWORD

Once in a generation, God raises up a man, taking him through the tests of time and faithfulness and into the "furnace of afflictions" — all in order to purify a mouthpiece for Himself. In this generation, that man has been none other than Bishop Paul S. Morton Sr.

Bishop Morton truly is a man of God who has the hand of God upon him. When a man goes through the kind of experiences that he has endured, very few ever make it back. Through all that Bishop Morton has encountered in his life and ministry, he is a living demonstration of Psalm 37:23-24:

> **The steps of a good man are ordered by the Lord: and he delighteth in his way. Though he fall, he shall not be utterly cast down: for the Lord upholdeth him with his hand.**

Bishop Morton has almost literally been to hell, yet he has been brought back by a mighty God and is willing to share his brokenness with the world.

Many in the body of Christ would rather cover up the broken and cracked areas of their lives, but this man of God understands that the anointing to minister to someone else flows out of those broken places of a person's life. I guarantee that everyone who reads this book will experience healing and victory because of one man's willingness to be transparent.

I am truly convinced that Bishop Morton is a gift to the body of Christ. I pray that as you read these pages, the anointing and presence of Almighty God would rest upon you. The wisdom that can be gleaned from this book is true life and spiritual healing. We can truly be grateful to God for the healing we have received from this man of integrity, who is willing to share with us what he has learned in the midst of his wilderness experience.

Bishop Eddie L. Long, D.D., D.H.L.
Senior Pastor
New Birth Missionary Baptist Church
Decatur, Georgia

INTRODUCTION

When a soda machine is out of order, they slap a sign on it so we know something's not right with it. But what happens when a preacher gets out of order? What happens when a man of God fails to follow God's order, when that man's thinking prevails over God's voice? What happens when a man allows his mind to tell his spirit what to do, rather than his spirit properly telling his mind what to do? I'll tell you what happens. Breakdown.

As a minister of the Gospel, my assignment in the kingdom of God is to preach the Good News of Jesus Christ and to destroy the works of the devil. I'd been doing that for years, but when the critical hour came, I found myself not ready for an intense bout of spiritual warfare because I was out of order. Spiritual warfare is mind over spirit or spirit over mind. Spiritual warfare started in the Garden of Eden. There were two trees, the Tree of Life, which represented the spirit, and the Tree of Knowledge of Good and Evil, which represented the mind. There was one command: Leave the Tree of Knowledge of Good and

Evil alone. In other words, don't lean to your mind, but to the spirit. If you do lean to the mind, you will be out of order and there will be a breakdown.

All of my life, I've tried to walk in humility. Arrogant people really turn me off. But after years in the ministry, at the height of my success, I began to stray from true humility. In fact, I began to boast in my humility, my integrity, and my honesty. I was in sin, coming short of the glory of God. There I was, with my head up in the air, boasting that I was not like some other preachers. "I don't do this and I don't do that," I bragged. I had become self-righteous like a Pharisee and, like a Pharisee, I had not realized it. But those whom God loves, He chastens. I was headed for a wilderness experience to be tested.

Now I know this sounds like a normal breakdown, where one goes back and forth between reality and the unknown, but it was not. God allowed it to appear to be a physical breakdown for several reasons. The first reason was to strip me of pride and to show me how I was nothing without Him. What appeared to be merely a physical breakdown to others was really God breaking me down so I could be taught spiritual lessons. Each time I would have what seemed like a "delusion episode," it would really be my classroom experience, the chastisement of my Teacher, and an engagement in spiritual warfare. After I had learned the lesson, I would come back to reality and share it with my wife. She was amazed. I was also amazed.

The second reason my experience had the appearance of a physical breakdown was that this was God's way of allowing the enemy to think he was winning. As soon as the enemy became convinced I was defeated, I learned my lesson, and God "plunged me to victory," on a new level, with more power. I've learned this: The wilderness experience has the appearance of defeat, but if successful, always delivers victory!

The wilderness is not a fun place to be — it is where God allows one to be tempted by the devil — but it is a place where God shows you the truth. By this temptation, God will reveal His truth and the truth about you. Through this experience, not only are your strengths manifested, but also your weaknesses. The success of this wilderness experience will depend upon you focusing your entire being on hearing and knowing the voice of the Holy Spirit and nothing else. His teaching, comfort, and healing power are your only way out of the wilderness and into the promised land.

Only when your flesh has been sufficiently reckoned dead and your spirit man has risen up strong inside, full of the Holy Spirit, will He lead you out of the wilderness to take the promised land. This time, you will be taking it not by your might, nor your power, but by the power of the Spirit of God.

PART ONE:

HOW MY KINGDOM FELL

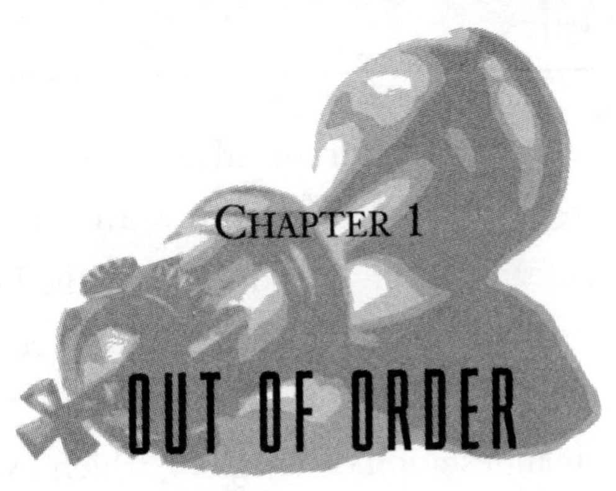

Chapter 1

OUT OF ORDER

The crisis began on a Thursday night when I was at home with my son, Paul Jr., and my youngest daughter, Christiann. My wife Debra was visiting our other daughter, Jasmine, in Atlanta. She called just to say, "Hi." I thank God for this woman of God. She knew immediately something was wrong with me and asked me what was going on. I couldn't see straight, I told her. I was dizzy. I saw demons that I felt were out to destroy me. It was frightening. I told Debra to pray because I was afraid. As she began to pray, I gained strength. Realizing I had entered into serious spiritual warfare and needed help, I told her I would call the elders of our church to come pray with me.

The warfare was so heavy, I began to do battle before the elders arrived — I couldn't wait. I quoted Scripture and prayed, fighting the devil with the Word. Two of my spiritual sons arrived first and joined me in the battle. The devil and I were fighting for my mind. He was so strong that there were moments when I didn't feel I would keep possession of my mind. But that night we won.

When Debra returned from Atlanta, she said she had been comforted by the Lord with this word: "If Paul were going to be defeated in any area of his life," the Lord said, "would the devil fight him so hard now? Of course not. He would just let the future take its course. But it is the fact that the manifestation of My glory, which I will show through the leadership of this man of God, is so great that the devil realizes he must go straight to the head to stop this mighty move of God."

In my home, we reveled in this spiritual victory. Four of my spiritual sons and I laughed and talked until about 2:00 a.m. Also, I had a good long talk with my son, comforting him because he'd been so frightened. He had never seen or heard me do spiritual warfare on that level. I told him that no matter how young or old you are, you must be totally serious about God, because demons are real. "If you're not built up in the Holy Ghost," I said, "the devil is going to knock you down and keep you down." Of course, my youngest daughter slept through the whole experience, as she often does when I preach!

TALKING IN CLASS

It all started with a newspaper article. The article reported an investment I had made for the Full Gospel Baptist Church Fellowship. I felt it was a good investment when I made it, but it turned out to be a bad one. The way the account was worded in the paper, it looked as though I didn't know what I was doing as a leader. I knew my church family would understand, because they had been with me over twenty years and knew I was a very capable leader. However, I had only been the Presiding Bishop for Full Gospel for a few years. What would they think?

Then there was the question of integrity. I had a good name and I did not want anyone to mess it up. The Bible says in Proverbs 22:1, **A good name is rather to be chosen than great riches, and loving favour rather than silver and gold.** Lately many Christians have been disappointed with leadership, and I was determined to be different. In that weakness of my pride, the devil saw an opening. He saw he could mess with my good name through that failed investment, and when he did my pride responded immediately. Although I was trying to live right and be an example of good spiritual leadership, I got caught up and became proud over my reputation. After the article was published, I publicly and privately tried to protect and defend my good name. So God had to remind me that He was in charge of keeping my name, not me. My goodness and righteousness were because of Jesus and Jesus alone.

God had to bring me back into order by teaching me a lesson. I had been very busy going to the wrong tree. He showed me there were two trees in the Garden of Eden, one was the Tree of Life and the other the Tree of the Knowledge of Good and Evil. The Tree of Life represented the rule of the spirit. The Tree of the Knowledge of Good and Evil represented the rule of human thinking, the mind. For this period, I had allowed my mind to rule instead of my spirit. I was out of order.

If I had been truly listening to the Holy Spirit in my spirit, I would have been spiritual. I would have heard and understood Jesus when He said in Matthew 6:24, **No man can serve two masters: for either he will hate the one, and love the other; or else he will hold to the one, and despise the other.** You cannot serve God and your carnal mind. Only one can be your master. If your mind rules over your spirit, then your mind is your master. If your spirit controls your mind, your spirit is your master. You must constantly kick the devil off the throne of your heart by listening to your spirit and obeying the voice of the Holy Spirit and God's Word over any humanistic, carnal thinking.

> **Therefore I say unto you, Take no thought for your life, what ye shall eat, or what ye shall drink; nor yet for your body, what ye shall put on. Is not the life more than meat, and the body than raiment?**
>
> **Matthew 6:25**

If the devil can find any opportunity, he will jump on the throne of your heart, and worrying is an open door to the enemy. I was disobedient to God's Word because my thoughts were filled with worry. I was worrying so much, my mind was racing and wouldn't stop. I couldn't eat. I couldn't sleep. And finally, I experienced breakdown.

During my breakdown, I was in a totally new, unknown realm. I was in a large classroom. There was a big stage with a long table and a lamp on the table. There was a big black curtain and a voice that always spoke from behind the curtain. His name was Holy Ghost and we were to address Him as Teacher. The only textbook we used was the Bible, and I was a babe in Christ. My lessons were how to be saved, how to be filled with the Holy Ghost, how to operate in the gifts of the Spirit, and how to cast out demons.

As the student, I was required to simply be quiet and listen, but the problem was, I was going back and forth from this unknown realm to the earthly realm. In the earthly realm, I already knew the things I was required to be taught over and over again in the unknown realm. Nevertheless, the command was clear: "Be quiet and listen." Still, I was disobedient. I would talk out because I had all the answers. I was out of order because I was not listening to the Spirit. Because my mind was ruling over

IF THE DEVIL CAN FIND ANY OPPORTUNITY, HE WILL JUMP ON THE THRONE OF YOUR HEART, AND WORRYING IS AN OPEN DOOR TO THE ENEMY. I WAS DISOBEDIENT TO GOD'S WORD BECAUSE MY THOUGHTS WERE FILLED WITH WORRY.

my spirit, I was kept in the wilderness longer than I wanted to be.

The Holy Spirit would begin to say something, but He would never get a chance to finish because I would begin to act immediately, before He could finish instructing me. When I acted in my own thinking, without hearing the full counsel of the Holy Spirit, He would stop speaking and the demons would take over. Now they were teaching, but I hadn't realized it.

For example, the Holy Spirit taught the lesson on spiritual weapons, that **the weapons of our warfare are not carnal, but mighty through God to the pulling down of strong holds** (2 Corinthians 10:4). But when my wife started talking to me about going to a doctor, that perhaps I needed medical help for a physical problem, I yelled, "No! Those are carnal weapons!" The demon was speaking and told me that it was the Holy Spirit. If only I would have thought about the rest of that passage:

> **Casting down imaginations, and every high thing that exalteth itself against the knowledge of God, and bringing into captivity every thought to the obedience of Christ.**
>
> **2 Corinthians 10:5**

That was exactly what I was failing to do, and I was losing the battle. I wasn't bringing my thoughts into captivity in obedience to Jesus Christ. Therefore, I began to come against the demons that I imagined were influencing Debra. The devil made me believe that doctors, who in reality were good, were actually bad. So I said, "Come out, demon!" over and over again, but I had no authority and the "demons" stayed there.

Frustrated, I went back to class and asked the teacher, the Holy Ghost, why I couldn't cast out these demons. "Because you don't listen," He said. "You jump ahead of Me because you think you have all the answers. If you stop trying to be the know-it-all preacher, you would know what to cast out and what to leave alone."

"Okay," I said, "I got it. I'm going to listen."

That Sunday morning, the third Sunday in February, I went to church. Debra brought a powerful message. She truly had a word from the Lord. Her text was Romans 14:17: **The kingdom of God is not meat and drink; but righteousness, and peace, and joy in the Holy Ghost.** I also shared my warfare experience against pride, fear, and self-pity, and my testimony of victory with my congregation.

Then the devil of deception, through the spirit of self, hit me again. When I got home, I began to rant and rave by quoting Scripture and searching for papers to defend myself in the investment failure. Debra started urging me to calm down because I needed rest. I said I was mad at the devil, but I was really mad at the spirit of self because I lost fellowship with God. I was failing to keep God's order. On the other hand, my flesh told me I couldn't fail. After all, I was The Pastor, I was The Bishop.

The fact was, I was exhausted and my mind and my body needed rest. For the first time in years, my wife and I didn't attend evening services. We rested. Not only was I exhausted physically, but because of my disobedience, I was also spiritually powerless. Because I thought I knew it all, because my thinking was prevailing over God's voice, I had lost fellowship with God. Because of the spirit of self, I couldn't fight the demonic voices that kept pestering me. My teacher, the Holy Ghost, tried to tell me, but I thought I knew it all. So I entered into "spiritual warfare" with my wife again.

Debra said, "Calm down. You need to rest. You have a church to pastor."

"Now Debra," I said, "you just preached that the kingdom of God is not meat and drink, but righteousness, peace, and joy in the Holy Ghost. The church is meat and drink. My family? Meat and drink." The devil was using Scripture to trick me, because he knows that my family and my church are parts of the kingdom that make me whole. Thank God for family and church. But that spirit of deception messed me up. I was rebuking the devil that I imagined was influencing my wife.

"You're coming out," I said. "You're focusing on food and drink and I've got righteousness and peace and joy in the Spirit." In fact, I had the total opposite. That's the way the devil works. He makes up seem to be down and down up. He makes good seem bad and bad good. Because of my disobedience, I didn't have righteousness; I had unrighteousness. I didn't have peace; I was restless. I didn't have joy; I was sad.

> **When he** [the devil] **lies, he speaks his native language, for he is a liar and the father of lies.**
>
> **John 8:44 NIV**

Jesus said it: The devil is the speaker of deceit. He is the father of lies. Because I was buying his lies, I couldn't resist his demons. Again, I went back to the Teacher, the Holy Ghost. "What happened?" I asked. "I want the kingdom. Debra was talking meat and drink. I was talking righteousness, joy, and peace in the Holy Ghost."

My Teacher said again, "Because you won't listen, because you know it all, you jump ahead of Me and make a fool of yourself." Listening to the devil will make any one of us act a fool. It's true. I was acting the fool.

A fool spurns his father's discipline, but whoever heeds correction shows prudence.

Proverbs 15:5 NIV

Sunday night I finally rested and felt God's peace again. Then on Monday I took off for the Bahamas. I was looking forward to a relaxing trip. I was just going to preach once, then I'd rest the remainder of the week. We landed, went to the hotel, and got ready for church. That's when the devil resumed his attack — with a vengeance. But because of my physical exhaustion and my lack of fellowship with the Holy Ghost, I didn't recognize the source of the attack.

In a vision, the devil talked to me as if he were the Holy Ghost. The vision was spiritual, but it was delusional. This devil is also a spirit. He instructed me to expose one of our Bishops of the Bahamas at the service. I saw this poor, innocent preacher as an enemy of God and therefore my enemy. The voice said that he was the enemy and I had to expose him that night. The demon said I should not mention it to anyone before the service, but to do it publicly during the service. *Yes, Holy Spirit,* I thought, *I will obey.*

When the service started, I approached the pulpit in the spirit. I had a true, Holy Spirit-led word from the Lord on insincere preachers — preachers with contracts, preachers out for money, and whoremongers in the pulpit. If I had just preached what the Spirit had given me, I would have been fine. But I'd had this vision, and the other spirit, the spirit of self, took over. I turned to this innocent preacher on the platform with me, pointed my foolish finger at him and said, "You are guilty!"

Without realizing it, I was having a breakdown right then. The devil had taken over at that point, and I could not see the Lord or recognize His voice. I had given in to the spirit of deception and he was in control. I made that man bow down. By the Spirit of God, I know this preacher is truly a man of God. Because of that, the devil hated him and wanted to embarrass him.

I say to everyone, please know that that was not the real me! I believe in respecting and honoring the man of God. The spirit of self had me because of my disobedience. I apologize to all of you. I'm so sorry. I know that the Spirit of God is love. He's compassionate, not rude. His Word says to be angry but sin not. (See Ephesians 4:26.) I would never have done that in my right mind. I should have known that God does not work out of order. In God's order, a preacher is always respected in his pulpit unless he is oppressed by demons. Even if what I'd seen in the vision had been true, I should have dealt with it differently.

JESUS SAID IT: THE DEVIL IS THE SPEAKER OF DECEIT. HE IS THE FATHER OF LIES. BECAUSE I WAS BUYING HIS LIES, I COULDN'T RESIST HIS DEMONS.

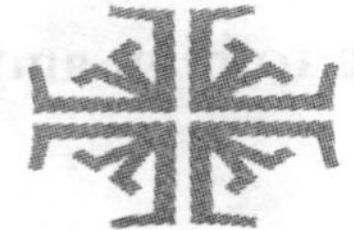

But even the archangel Michael, when he was disputing with the devil over the body of Moses, did not dare to bring a slanderous accusation against him, but said, "The Lord rebuke you!"

Jude 9 NIV

Of course, what happened to me had to happen publicly. It was a lesson for me in disobedience and pride. The embarrassment I suffered was to teach me a lesson because of the special assignment God had given me. "Learn the lesson," He said, "learn the lesson well, and be sure you listen. In this unknown realm, you must hear Me. You must learn My voice. You don't know it all. Don't jump ahead of Me and you won't make a fool of yourself." I was beginning to get the message. Kingdoms fall when man's thinking prevails over God's voice.

A LESSON ON SERVING

Now it came to pass, as they went, that he [Jesus] **entered into a certain village: and a certain woman named Martha received him into her house.**

And she had a sister called Mary, which also sat at Jesus' feet and heard his word.

But Martha was cumbered about with much serving, and came to him, and said, Lord, dost

thou not care that my sister hath left me to serve alone? bid her therefore that she help me.

And Jesus answered and said unto her, Martha, Martha, thou art careful and troubled about many things:

But one thing is needful: and Mary hath chosen that good part, which shall not be taken away from her.

Luke 10:38-42

Jesus was very close to the family of Mary, Martha, and their brother Lazarus. Every time He passed through Bethany, He stayed in their home. Not only were they special friends, but I believe He also enjoyed Martha's cooking. In Luke 10:39, Mary seemed to be the complete opposite of her sister Martha. In Martha's eyes, Mary didn't seem to be concerned about being a good hostess to Jesus and Martha could not handle it. She finally expressed her irritation to Jesus. As far as she was concerned, Mary was lazy and out of order.

Martha seemed to be confident in her role and in her ability to perform in that role. She was confident that what she was doing was right. She was a good cook, a good hostess, and she knew it. If there was a very special guest that the family wanted to impress, they'd ask Martha to cook, and although Jesus was their friend, He was also a celebrity. Everybody had heard about Him. He drew big crowds wherever He went. There was something very special about Him. He had an anointing and He preached like no one else. He had opened many blind eyes and deaf ears. So when He came to their home, Martha really wanted to make an impression. This particular time she was trying to show off her best meal and she expected her sister Mary to do her part.

Martha was annoyed that Mary was just sitting there at Jesus' feet listening instead of helping her cook. She'd probably given Mary a few stern glares and not-so-subtle hints that she needed help. Finally Martha couldn't stand it anymore and complained to Jesus, "Lord, don't You even care that my sister has me working in the kitchen all by myself? Tell her to get herself into this kitchen right this second!"

At that moment there was spiritual warfare going on. Martha's mind was fighting the Holy Spirit. Her thinking was prevailing over God's voice. Martha was doing what was right in the natural world, but Mary was doing what was right in the spirit world. The great spiritual truths that Jesus was teaching to Mary and the others were of infinitely greater value than the meat and drink Martha was preparing, but Martha couldn't see that.

Not only that, Martha felt she was so right in her serving role that she felt fully justified in telling Jesus what to do. Her thinking, prevailing over God's voice, had her ordering Jesus to tell Mary to come help her in the kitchen. She was so out of order that she felt it was perfectly right to have Jesus straighten Mary out in the matter.

But Jesus, instead of correcting Mary, told Martha she was worrying too much. In essence, He was saying "You have no peace; you need to calm down. I'll keep you in perfect peace if you keep your mind focused on Me. (See Isaiah 26:3.) Stop trying so hard to impress Me and let Me show you something wonderful about the kingdom of God."

For my thoughts are not your thoughts, neither are your ways my ways, saith the Lord.

Isaiah 55:8

Does that ring a bell? Like Martha, too many of us try to show the Lord what we know, how well we can sing, how well we can preach, or how hard we work in ministry. But His thoughts are far higher than our thoughts, and His ways higher than our ways. What we really need to do is quit Martha-ing around and start acting like Mary, sitting at Jesus' feet. Like Mary, we must listen to the Spirit and allow the Lord to show us what to do. Mary realized that she needed to hear every word Jesus had to say, so she was at His feet. Lunch could wait. Mary was receiving spiritual food that would last.

It doesn't matter how good we are at something or how busy we get, we must always hear what God has to say first. Yes, if Jesus hadn't been speaking, Mary could have been up helping Martha. It would have been a time for both to serve Him. But when Jesus speaks, we need to stop whatever we're doing, sit down, and listen.

That's exactly the lesson the Holy Spirit had to teach me. I, like Martha, was confident in my service to the Lord. I knew how to "cook well" in ministry. It was my gift, and I was using my gift to serve the Lord. But I got so wrapped up in using my gift that I failed to heed the voice of God. God was telling me to sit and listen, but I was busy serving and cooking. God had to deal with me to show me that the one thing needful in my life was to sit down. His ways are higher than my ways. His words must prevail over my thinking, no matter how service-minded I got.

God had something to say. He told me, "Paul, you don't need to cook right now. I have other cooks. Greater St. Stephen will be fine and the Full Gospel Baptist Church Fellowship will be fine. Sit at My feet for forty days so you can hear clearly what I'm saying. Sit at My feet, and when you get up, you can share the lessons you learn in a book to help the people of God."

Well, I finally listened. I turned the kitchen over to others and sat down at His feet for forty days. I was admitted to a facility and given godly help for body, mind, and spirit. For those forty days God ministered to me. It was quality time — Spirit over mind time — time for only the Lord and me.

I listened attentively and He instructed me every step of the way. He told me exactly what to write in this book. He even gave me songs to write. I wrote about nine songs in one day. I heard the Spirit with so much clarity it was amazing. I could hear Him speaking really well — no other voice seemed to matter. Not only did He give me the words to the songs, but He also gave me the tune for each song. All because I stayed at His feet awhile.

Have you ever considered that God has other cooks who can tend to your kitchen? Have you seen that the "one thing needful" is to sit at the feet of Jesus? Oh yes, we do get up like Martha and we work, but what God is saying is that we must know when to cook and when to sit and listen. When we go through trials, it's not going to matter how much cooking we have done. We'll stand or fall based on how much time we've spent sitting at the feet of Jesus being fed.

If we will sit at the feet of Jesus, we will not get out of order.

Chapter 2

God Sends a Cloud

I was out of order. As a result of allowing my thinking to prevail over God's voice, playing Martha's role rather than that of Mary, I was led by the Lord into the wilderness for forty days. It was very similar to the experience Jesus faced in Matthew 4:1 TLB.

Then Jesus was led out into the wilderness by the Holy Spirit, to be tempted there by Satan.

Jesus went into the wilderness willingly, out of obedience. I, however, went into the wilderness because of my disobedience. "Then Paul Morton was led into the wilderness!"

The wilderness is a portion of land that is unused or has not yet been cultivated. It was into the wilderness, the unused land of my mind, that the Spirit led me to teach me several vital lessons. As God would have it, the plan was for me to go there and be tempted by the devil because of my disobedience. And tempted I was, but God was in control.

The disobedience that set me up for my wilderness experience was allowing my own thinking to get out of sync with God's order. Throughout my years in the ministry, I had always believed in following God's order. I would rebuke the devil if he tempted me to get out of order. However, when I faced a situation in my life where it looked as if God was moving too slowly to bring things into His proper order, I took matters into my own hands. Intending to do good for the kingdom of God, I said to myself, "I know how to handle this, Lord. I know what to do and how to do it."

I didn't realize the significance of what I was saying. It sounded like "God talk," but I was out of order. How? My mind (self-consciousness) was telling my spirit man (God-consciousness) what to do, instead of my spirit man telling my mind what to do. When this happens to Christians, we experience a breakdown in God's proper order. My mind was out of order because of my disobedience.

After returning to New Orleans from the Bahamas, God continued to deal with me mightily. Throughout that week the Holy Spirit taught me lessons and allowed me to have experiences dealing with obedience, deception, humility, and fully understanding the Word of God. There were times when Debra and I would pray for a few minutes and at times for an hour before we got a breakthrough.

After each battle we would cry tears of joy and of sadness, because in the unknown realm, sometimes I won the battles and other times I was deceived, disobedient, or confused. God was teaching me how to win against the devil by being sensitive to His voice only. If I listened to Him and obeyed Him, I would be victorious over the devil every time.

Through all this spiritual fighting, I was becoming exhausted in my body because the enemy would not allow me to sleep. Although I didn't agree at first, Debra and two of my bishops took me to a hospital. She did not want to be deceived by the devil and allow something physical to go untreated. Thank God an examination revealed nothing physically wrong.

While I was being checked at the local hospital, Debra and those who were very close to us searched for a place where I could get rest and help, but a place that was also attuned to the spiritual aspects of my problem. They located several, but I would have to share a room with another person, which would totally stress me out. In the end, we decided to trust God for my healing.

At this point, Debra was too tired to argue with me about sharing a room, and she knew I needed rest, so we all retired to the nearest hotel. It was about 5:30 in the morning. After a few hours of sleep, I woke up with much to share with Debra. I began to tell her things that had stressed me out. I told her that I didn't need to be in the hospital because I had gone inside myself and pulled out what had got to me.

I also began to share other lessons God had taught me. I said God had given me a boldness to deal with situations and a sensitivity to know exactly what was going on in many instances. I said the Holy Spirit had showed me that I kept making the mistake of going ahead of Him. I told her that God had taken me to an unknown realm where I was as innocent as a child. In that realm I had power from God, but like a child I didn't know what to do with it. Being inexperienced, I'd misused and abused the power and had to be taught by God how to handle it.

Then I stopped and told Debra that I needed to share those lessons with her. God had also told me that she would share with me in the ministry of deliverance and spiritual warfare. I instructed her to go eat and get the things she needed to do out of the way, because the next discussion would require her full attention.

After lunch, we held hands and prayed, and then we began to sing praise to God. Weeping, I took the Bible and opened it to Jesus' wilderness experience and began to explain. I told Debra that, for now, she was not supposed to talk at all, not even to ask a question, because of the unfamiliarity of the subject matter. After a long period of teaching I stopped, saying that God said I should tell her the lesson in parts, since what I'd shared with her was all that she could handle then. She remarked later how relieved she was. It was intense.

By that point, it was dinnertime. We got ready and ate with my assistants in the hotel's restaurant. After dinner, I left them and went up to the room because I felt it was too chilly in the restaurant. It was the trick of the enemy to get me alone. Debra soon felt something in the spirit and asked Elder Love to come with her to the room where I was resting.

As they entered, Debra saw that the room was dark except for the light from the television. She called out my name and I answered her. She was relieved when she heard my voice because she could tell I was all right from the sound of my voice. We talked a minute then said goodnight. The television was left on.

Debra fell asleep for about fifteen to thirty minutes. Then she turned to put her arm across my chest and felt my heart beating at an accelerated rate. She saw that I was looking at some scary-looking animals on CNN. She called my name, but I did not respond. She saw that I was in a daze, looking in the direction of the animals, and she began to pray.

It was spiritual warfare again. The devil had dispatched demons to keep me from resting and the deaf and dumb spirit was also oppressing me. Debra recognized them and began to call them off, praying and quoting the Word. Eventually I came out of it. She told me that although she was fighting for me spiritually, she also felt there was something physical that needed attention. I needed to get an extended period of rest. People of God, and especially leaders, must learn how to admit that.

We got into the car and drove back to the facility. I silently held Debra's hand as I stared out the window. There was a little fear, but then a quiet word of comfort was spoken in our midst, "I will never leave you nor forsake you." As I checked in and Debra sadly got ready to leave me, I said, "D, we have to trust God. This is what I need; I'm going to be fine."

And I was. During that time, many generational curses surfaced, hidden fears were exposed, and life-changing decisions were made. I had time alone to discover things about myself. I had time to be honest with myself about the part I'd played in my stress attack, even concerning my relationship with Debra and our family.

GOD'S LESSON ON THE CLOUDS

This Holy Ghost-filled man, this anointed preacher and bishop, should have known better. But all the devil

DEBRA . . . FELT THERE WAS SOMETHING PHYSICAL THAT NEEDED ATTENTION. I NEEDED TO GET AN EXTENDED PERIOD OF REST. PEOPLE OF GOD, AND ESPECIALLY LEADERS, MUST LEARN HOW TO ADMIT THAT.

needs is a little space, a little crack in the armor. He worked on my weakness and slipped in, but the devil better look out now! He messed up. He messed with my mind and I'm glad he did. He meant it for evil, but God turned it around for good, because my experiences will prevent others from falling for the same lies.

This was an important lesson for me from God, and it had to be made public, because God wanted to use it to bless others. We overcome by the blood of the Lamb and by *the words of our testimony.* (See Revelation 12:11.) When we go through tests in our lives, we learn that we have the faith we need to endure even greater trials. But many times God wants others to know we have faith. Well, how is He going to reveal our faith to others? He sends clouds.

> **Wherein ye greatly rejoice, though now for a season, if need be, ye are in heaviness through manifold temptations:**
>
> **That the trial of your faith, being much more precious than of gold that perisheth, though it be tried with fire, might be found unto praise and honour and glory at the appearing of Jesus Christ.**
>
> **1 Peter 1:6-7**

This scripture passage makes it clear that all of us must face trials, and that many times we will experience heaviness through the trials we face. But it's for a glorious reason: because the trial of our faith is much more precious than gold. God has a purpose. He wants us to be tried in the fire so that we might be found unto praise and honor and glory at the appearing of Jesus Christ. Whatever situation we go through, we must give Him the praise.

Now, how is God going to reveal this faith of ours to others? He must send a cloud. Imagine we're looking up into the night sky and seeing the moon. We wouldn't pay much attention to the plain, simple moon. It's nothing unusual. But what if we look up and see the moon peeking out from behind clouds as they pass by. What a beautiful sight that is! Why is it so beautiful now? The brightness of the moon is much more noticeable as it interacts with the clouds around it. The darkness actually reveals its beauty.

That's what God will do with our faith. Many of us would just have plain, simple faith if it were not for the clouds in our lives. The clouds that God allows to form, the troubles we go through, are what God uses to reveal our faith to others so that we can have a testimony. That's what happened to Job.

If it weren't for the clouds in Job's life, we wouldn't have a sermon to preach about him. We'd just say Job was born, Job lived by faith, and Job died. But this is not the case. What catches our attention is the fact that Job's faith underwent terrible trials — nasty dark clouds in his life.

You may know the story. Satan went up into the heavens and God said to him, "Where have you been?"

Satan responded: "Oh, just going to and fro in the earth." In other words, he was looking for somebody he could devour.

God said, "Have you considered My servant, Job? There's nobody like him in all the land. He fears Me and runs from evil."

Satan replied, "Well sure he serves You, considering the way You've surrounded him with a hedge of protection and blessed the work of his hands and everything he has. He's rich! But if You allow me to take all Job has, I guarantee You he will curse You! He won't want anything to do with You!"

"Go ahead, try Job," God said.

So Satan did. He destroyed everything Job had. His enemies took his cattle and his oxen. Job had been the richest man in the land of Ur, and suddenly he was dead broke. Still, he wouldn't sin by blaming God for his troubles.

But Satan wasn't satisfied, so he decided to take Job's family. Satan thought that surely Job's faith would break when he lost all of his children at once. But what happened? Job's faith was revealed for the public to see. With his fortune gone and his children dead, he declared, "The Lord gives and the Lord takes away. Blessed be the name of the Lord." (See Job 1:6-22.) Faith shined from the clouds.

Satan still wasn't satisfied, so he tried to destroy Job's flesh, expecting the pain to break his faith. Before long, Job was sitting in ashes, covered with boils from the top of his head to the soles of his feet. He had to mash ashes into the sores to ease the pain.

Job's wife, tired of seeing Job in pain, said, "Why don't you just curse God and die?" But then came his faith, visible to everyone from behind even darker clouds. "You speak like a foolish woman. Should we receive good from the Lord and not bad?" (See Job 2:1-10.) Job knew it and we must know it: it's only a test. Even from his sick bed, he looked past the devil, and the light of his faith crept out from behind the clouds.

Some people go through trials but they fail the test. God wants to reveal our faith in Him to others by our reaction to our trials. We cannot allow the devil to get the victory by not passing a test.

Consider Abraham. Late in his life, he finally had the son he'd desired all his life. He knew it was a promise kept by God. But suddenly there comes a command from the Lord, "Take now your son, your only son, Isaac, whom you love and offer him as a sacrifice." This was serious spiritual warfare.

Lord, Abraham thought, *I hear what You are saying, but I waited one hundred years for this miracle! You can't be serious! If I lose Isaac, there will be no more hope.*

But Abraham knew the voice of God and would not ignore it. His mind did not matter. His mind came under the Spirit, his fears fell below his faith, and his faith shined through the cloud. So Abraham and Isaac headed up to the top of the mountain, a place where they made sacrifices to the Lord.

Isaac was probably so helpful to his father because Abraham was so old. I can imagine him saying as he gathered the wood and built the altar, "Daddy, everything is ready, the altar, the wood, and the fire, but where is the sacrifice?"

Can you imagine how Abraham must have felt as he had to tell his son, whom he loved so much, that *he* was to be the sacrifice. Well, Isaac knew that Abraham was close to the Lord. With the strength of youth that he had, I'm sure that he had the strength to overpower his father. But Isaac was obedient and lay on the altar as Abraham bound his hands and his feet.

MANY OF US WOULD JUST HAVE PLAIN, SIMPLE FAITH IF IT WERE NOT FOR THE CLOUDS IN OUR LIVES.

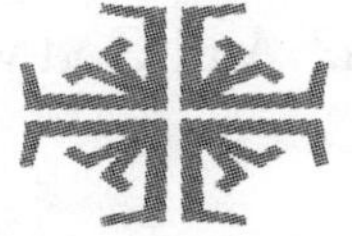

Abraham heard from the Lord and he chose to obey divine order. He picked up the knife, ready to plunge it into his son's chest. But suddenly he heard a voice from heaven: "Stay your hand, Abraham. Hold up, it's only a test." Before He established a nation of chosen people through him, God had to see if Abraham was in divine order, with Spirit over mind, with faith over feelings.

Abraham could have easily said, "No way! I have my son now and I'm not going to lose him for anybody!" Instead, he obeyed the voice of God. We must always hear the voice of God *and obey*. Then, in the midst of the cloud, our faith will be revealed. God revealed Abraham's faith through the cloud, and generations have seen his faith shining from the pages of the Bible.

In the same way, God wants to reveal our faith through our trials. So often we fail the tests God puts before us because we allow our minds to prevail over the Holy Spirit. Why are we surprised when tests come? We all should understand by now that eventually our faith will be put to the test. The question is whether our faith will be revealed in such a way that pleases God. Too often people complain, crying that their test is so hard. Their faith is forgotten. All they can see is the cloud, the trial. To overcome, to survive the trial intact, we must say "Lord, reveal my faith." And God will be there for you.

Not only will God reveal your faith by what you go through, He will also strengthen your faith. We mature in our faith and strengthen our faith by going through all of the seasons of life's trials and blessings. To illustrate, imagine that our faith is a tree, growing through the seasons. If there's sunshine all the time or rain all the time, the tree would not grow well. If it was cold all the time or hot all the time, the tree would not grow well. Its roots would die and the least wind would blow it down. God allows us to go through all the seasons to strengthen us. I had that kind of experience in my own life.

In 1989, we had the coldest winter ever in New Orleans. In my front yard I had several beautiful palm trees, and I loved my palm trees! Right in the city of New Orleans, I had a taste of Hawaii. But this winter, this *cold* winter, my poor palm trees could not stand the freezing temperatures. My poor palm trees had not experienced the cycle of the seasons. They'd only known warm weather.

Right across the street there was an old oak tree. No matter how cold it got, that tree still stood. That old oak tree had cousin oak trees in Chicago, New York, and Detroit, and was well-rooted in the hard cycle of the seasons. Oak trees stand firm through all the seasons. Let me tell you, my brothers and sisters, we must be spiritual oak trees.

I found out, in moving to the city of New Orleans, that I was a palm tree. I wasn't used to the trials that came with the seasons of life. I moved to New Orleans when I was just 22 years old. Back home, my family was well respected and people loved me and cared for me. To them, I was their preacher's boy who'd grown up in their church and they were proud of me. It was all warm weather — I didn't have to experience the seasons.

But when I moved to New Orleans, God allowed me to pastor at Greater St. Stephen. I joined Greater St. Stephen and in six months I became the Assistant Pastor. A year and a half later, the pastor of the church died in an accident. Suddenly there was a chill in the air because of the rapid growth of the church.

Here I was, a young man, a palm tree, wanting to do the will of God. I did my best, but still people started talking about me. They started lying about me and I could not understand it. I would go to my room and cry, "Lord, why? I'm doing my best. Why are people lying?" I wasn't ready for this sudden winter.

But my enemies made one mistake: they kept on lying about me. The more they lied, the more I prayed. Prayer was strengthening me. What the devil meant for evil, God was using for good. God was changing me from a palm tree to an oak tree so that I would be able to deal with all of the seasons.

Consider it pure joy, my brothers, whenever you face trials of many kinds,

because you know that the testing of your faith develops perseverance.

Perseverance must finish its work so that you may be mature and complete, not lacking anything.

James 1:2-4 NIV

Let me tell you, this is the stability and strength God wants in your life. Too many of us want sunshine all the time, but if we have all good we won't be able to deal with the bad when it comes. We need to experience both the good and the bad to strengthen us. That's what God was doing with me. He was strengthening my faith for the storms to come. A palm tree would have been blown away into the Gulf of Mexico by the storm I experienced during my breakdown. But the seasons of life had made me a tough, old oak tree, and I survived with just a few dead branches lost to the wind.

When I look back upon the entire ordeal with my breakdown, I see the light of God's love shining through that cloud. I see the light of my faith shining through, sometimes faintly, but ultimately dispelling the cloud of darkness that sought to destroy me. By the blood of the Lamb and the word of this testimony, I overcome — now and in the future — every attack and scheme of the enemy.

Chapter 3

The Dangers of Disobedience

At the very core of the lessons I learned during my breakdown was one that God showed me through the story of King Saul's disobedience in 1 Samuel 15. Through the prophet Samuel, God had commanded him to totally destroy Israel's idol-worshipping enemy, the Amalekites. He was to kill the king, every man, woman, and child, and even destroy every animal. And that's what Saul did — well, almost.

Saul thought it would be a better idea to keep the Amalekite king, Agag, and the best of the sheep and oxen to sacrifice to God. He would kill everything else as God commanded. It certainly seemed like a good idea at the time. Maybe he thought he was improving on God's idea, but it wasn't what God wanted.

As a result, God told Samuel the prophet that He was sorry He ever made Saul king, because this was not the first time Saul had refused to obey Him. Samuel was so deeply moved when he heard God's voice that he cried to the Lord all night. Early the next morning, he went to find Saul. Someone said that he had gone to Mount Carmel to erect a monument to himself and had then gone on to Gilgal.

When Samuel finally found him, Saul greeted him cheerfully. "Bless you, Samuel," he said, "I've carried out the Lord's command."

"Really? Then what was all the bleating of sheep and lowing of oxen I heard?" Samuel asked.

"Uh, well, the people spared the best of the sheep and oxen," Saul admitted. "But just so they can sacrifice them to the Lord our God. We've destroyed everything else."

Then Samuel said to Saul, "Stop! Listen to what the Lord told me last night. When you didn't think much of yourself, God made you king of Israel. He sent you to completely destroy the sinners, the Amalekites, until they were all dead. Then why didn't you obey the Lord? Why did you rush for the loot and do evil in the sight of the Lord?"

"But I *have* obeyed the Lord," Saul insisted. "I did what He told me. I brought King Agag but killed everyone else. And it was only when my troops demanded it that I let them keep the best of the sheep, oxen, and other loot to sacrifice to the Lord."

Samuel replied, "Has the Lord as much pleasure in your burnt offerings and sacrifices as in your obedience? *Obedience is far better than sacrifice.* God wants you to obey Him. Since you have rejected the commandment of the Lord, He has rejected you as king."

As Samuel turned to go, Saul grabbed at him to try to hold him back. Samuel's robe tore. Samuel said to him, "See? The Lord has torn the kingdom of Israel from you today and He has given it to a countryman of yours who is better than you are. He who is the Glory of Israel is not lying nor will He change His mind, for He is not a man."

The Amalekites, whom God told Saul to destroy, had been the enemy of the children of Israel for a very long time. They fought them continuously. But fighting God's chosen people is dangerous. Fighting God's anointed is risky.

> **And David said to Abishai, Destroy him not: for who can stretch forth his hand against the Lord's anointed, and be guiltless?**
>
> **1 Samuel 26:9**

God got tired of the Amalekites. He will allow the enemy to fight you for awhile, but eventually He will say, "That's enough." God told Saul to destroy them completely. He wanted all of those evil people dead, and

He wanted Saul and his army to do it. It was a blessing to be chosen by God to fulfill this assignment.

It is a privilege to be able to say, "God chose me." But some people can't handle the blessings of God. Instead of being humbled by them, many become lifted up in pride. Consequently, we begin to allow our pride to move us away from the will of God. We begin to forget who's in charge, following our own thinking right into disobedience.

This sin of disobedience is something else! The Lord told Samuel He was sorry He had ever made Saul king and blessed him. He saw that Saul didn't know how to handle blessings. He had refused to obey God, and God sent Samuel to tell him how He felt. Thank God for the prophet who will tell you how God feels about your disobedience!

When Samuel tracked Saul down, Saul greeted the prophet cheerfully, telling him that he'd carried out the Lord's command. He thought he'd done exactly what the Lord had told him to do. Saul was not alone in his error. Many people still respond that same way, because it's possible to fool ourselves into thinking that we have done what God said. We know we haven't completed exactly what God has told us in exactly the way He said, but we've managed to convince ourselves that we have done the right thing because of our own wisdom or experience. Unbelievable!

WE BEGIN TO FORGET WHO'S IN CHARGE, FOLLOWING OUR OWN THINKING RIGHT INTO DISOBEDIENCE.

Then the animals exposed Saul's lie to Samuel. "If you did exactly what God told you, then what's that I hear? It sounds like bleating sheep and lowing oxen," said Samuel. There are still people who insist that they've done exactly what God told them to do, but the evidence exposes their lie. "I stopped drinking," but you can smell liquor on their breath. "I'm not having sex," but a month later she's pregnant. We say we're being faithful to God, yet the evidence gives us away. *Then* we confess. Confession rarely comes until we get caught!

Listen to Saul confess after the sound of the sheep and oxen gave him away — and then try to excuse his sin. "It's true, the army spared the best sheep and oxen, but we're giving them to the Lord your God, Samuel."

We say, "This is for You, God," when we get caught at the casino. "If I win I'm going to give so much to the church." Or maybe we say, "Well, I was just witnessing to that girl in that bar so my wife and I could take her to church."

God's no fool. That's nothing but "got-caught talk." Our flesh and selfish ambition would rather disobey God than kill the best sheep. We tell the Lord, "Oh, look what we're going to do for You. This sheep is for You." But actually it's for us. The reason we try to persuade God to let us keep the best sheep is because we see how it will benefit us. Most of the time it's to satisfy our flesh. "I'm living common law, but I bring my old lady to church. I go out to nightclubs, but some of those same people may come to church with me." No! God said to slay *utterly.*

KILL THE KING

Saul said, "I know we were to kill everybody, but I kept the king." Keeping a king that was to be destroyed will keep you out of order. As long as that rebellious king is there, he will reign. Kill him! What king is still alive in your life that should be dead? If you have kept the king of rebellion alive in your heart, that is as bad as the sin of witchcraft. Rebellion will control your mind and have you doing things that you would not normally do. It will cause your mind to reign over your spirit instead of the Holy Spirit being in control.

If the king of stubbornness still reigns in your heart, the Bible says that it's as if you worshipped idols. The Holy Spirit will remind you that you should have no other gods before Him, but your stubborn mind will say, "Not so. I know what's right, but I don't care." The Spirit will say, "You are wrong. You should repent and apologize." Yet you will say, "I know I should but I'm not going to." The king of stubbornness has you.

If there is anything reigning over your life other than the King of kings, you should kill it. If you are keeping a king you should have killed, please utterly destroy it. Saul kept a king that was supposed to die. He was disobedient, and as a result, he lost his promised blessing.

Saul tried to impress God with what he had to offer, thinking a live king was better than a dead king. He tried to impress Him by keeping the best sheep to sacrifice, but God spoke clearly, "Your obedience is better than a sacrifice." He still desires us to listen to Him and obey Him rather than to try to impress Him.

Samuel said, "You rejected the Word of Jehovah and He has rejected you from being king." When we reject Him, we no longer have authority. "Lord, I disobeyed Your instructions; therefore, I am void of authority and power. I was afraid of the people and I did what they demanded," confessed Saul. But it was too late. His authority was gone. The Word says Saul pleaded with Samuel to pardon him and go with him and worship. But Samuel told Saul it was no use. "Because you have rejected the commandment of the Lord, He has rejected you from being king."

Well, that was the Law under the old covenant. But thank the Lord we are under the new covenant, which gives us God's grace because of Jesus' death on the cross.

When we sin, we can repent, turn away from our wrong-doing, and ask the Lord to pardon us in the name of Jesus. Then we can go and worship Him. It is only when we recognize and yield to God's authority that He gives us our authority.

The Word says that as Samuel turned to go away, Saul grabbed at him to try to hold him back and he tore Samuel's robe. It was a prophetic action. Samuel said, "See, the Lord has torn the kingdom of Israel from you today and has given it to a someone who is better than you are." Because of Saul's disobedience, the Lord had taken his crown, his blessings, and his authority and given them to a better man.

This is what God will do in our lives if we do not kill the kings of rebellion, pride, lust, greed, or anything else that is an abomination to Him. Sometimes He will take that with which He has blessed us and give it to someone who is better than us because they listen to His voice and obey Him.

How many times do we hear Him but shut Him out? How many times do we listen to Him and still do not obey what He tells us to do?

My friend, don't allow someone else to get your blessing because of your hardheaded disobedience. If you do, you have no one to blame but yourself. The blessing was yours, but you lost it because you refused to obey His voice. Why not sacrifice your will by obeying His voice and keep your blessing?

Like Saul, I was also chastised by God. But unlike Saul, God gave me another chance before He took my blessing away. I had a wilderness experience, a breakdown. As God broke me down in this experience, like Saul I learned that we must listen to *everything* God says and *exactly* what God says. We must not rationalize it, try to improve on it, or look for a way to wiggle out. We must simply take action. When we don't respond, we don't obey. When we don't obey, we open a door for the devil to attack.

WEAPONS OF WAR

As Christians, we must understand that if we obey God, we will encounter spiritual warfare. Demons are going to attack and we must be ready to fight until they are defeated. Christians have no neutral ground. We can say we don't want to hear about demons, but we might as well save our breath. If we're on God's side, we're against Satan and we're going to rumble. We *will* do spiritual warfare.

In order to do spiritual warfare successfully, we must go through training. Believers are trained in different

Christians have no neutral ground. We can say we don't want to hear about demons, but we might as well save our breath. If we're on God's side, we're against Satan and we're going to rumble.

ways, and those experiences serve as warfare training for us. In the experience I went through, I seemed to be reliving Philippians 3:10:

> **That I may know him and the power of his resurrection, and the fellowship of his sufferings, being made conformable unto his death.**

I was being conformed like never before! God was renewing my life and delivering me from my sins, which the enemy had camouflaged in my life. I was going through boot camp. In boot camp, young men and women give up their old lives of civilian individuality to be reborn as effective fighting soldiers. We must also die to our old ways to become effective members of the body of Christ.

> **Therefore we are buried with him by baptism into death: that like as Christ was raised up from the dead by the glory of the Father, even so we also should walk in newness of life.**
>
> **Romans 6:4**

Adam messed us up. Mankind was free from sin but Adam and Eve decided they were going to do what God told them not to do. From then on, mankind has been living under a curse spiritually, mentally, and physically.

The only way to come out from under that curse is for us to die to ourselves and be reborn in Jesus Christ.

Before I continue, I want to take a moment to ask you: Are you sure of your relationship with God? Do you know you've been saved by the shed blood of Jesus Christ? We can't run a race until we're on the right track. If your relationship with God has been based on merely going to church or shaking a preacher's hand, or if you've never even darkened the door of a church but realize you need a real relationship with the living God, it's natural to ask, "What must I do to be saved?"

Here's the answer:

> **If you confess with your mouth, "Jesus is Lord," and believe in your heart that God raised him from the dead, you will be saved.**
>
> **For it is with your heart that you believe and are justified, and it is with your mouth that you confess and are saved.**
>
> **Romans 10:9-10 NIV**

Being a Christian is not religion, church membership, or the work you do for God or man. It's simply faith in the fact that God raised His Son Jesus from the dead and the verbal confession before others that He is your Lord.

Don't let man's traditions rob you of this simple yet powerful truth from God's Word.

If you are a backslider, someone who has been born again but has left fellowship with God to follow their own ways, you need to repent. That means to turn away from the ways of the world and return to God and His way. If you haven't been living in God's order, walking in His Word, and listening to His voice, demons have been reigning in your life and Satan has had a ball. Leave the party now, while you still have your immortal soul.

Perhaps you've been a Christian for some time, but you're seeking a deeper relationship with God, a more victorious walk in the Spirit. You want His perfect will to be done in your life. You've been through trials in your life, the seasons of cold and hot, and you're becoming a mighty oak of faith, yet you want to be made even tougher, to be made more ready by God for any storm.

No matter what stage of the Christian walk you're in right now, it's time for the showdown. It's time for warfare. Are you ready to fight?

Although we're born again only once, to be effective Christians we need to die daily to our fleshly ways by our complete faith and trust in God. Our dying will allow us to be conformed not only to Jesus' death, but also to His resurrection, and thereby stay out of the wilderness. The power of that resurrection will make us powerful, effective witnesses for Him. It will allow God's voice to prevail over our thinking and keep us in God's order.

Just as a soldier's life is governed by a code of conduct, a new commitment will bring new demands upon us, a higher standard of life and duty. We can't keep up with these demands or measure up to these standards all by ourselves. We need the fullness of the Holy Spirit. If you are saved, ask the Lord to fill you with His Holy Spirit.

To cooperate with the infilling of the Holy Spirit, you must make room for Him. You should see less of you and more of Him. If you're going to be prepared for spiritual warfare, you need the fullness of the Holy Spirit — His power to be an overcomer, power over the enemy, and power over your weaknesses. We are empowered by the Holy Spirit for the task.

Seal the power of the Holy Spirit with a builder-upper, the edifier — our heavenly language or prayer language. This enables us to stay empowered while engaging in spiritual warfare. Our heavenly language edifies and builds us up. Yes, we are filled, and we are overcomers, but we stay filled with the help of our heavenly language.

Just as soldiers have special weapons for special situations, in spiritual warfare, we need the gifts of the Spirit. Four main ones for spiritual warfare are the word of knowledge, the word of wisdom, the gift of discerning of spirits, and the gift of faith. Properly equipped with salvation and the Holy Spirit, we can overcome the devil with the Word of God and get ourselves in order.

Getting ourselves in God's order means obedience. This is so simple, but it can be difficult. We can be born again. We can be filled with the Holy Spirit. We can read and study God's Word. We can pray in the Spirit and listen to what He tells us. But all of this spiritual activity becomes totally fruitless and worthless if we do not obey Him.

On the other hand, if we practice all these things and then obey Him, there is no limit to what God can accomplish in and through our lives.

Chapter 4

God's Order

Whenever a war is being waged, more than any other time, we all must choose either God's order or man's disorder. I was clearly not ministering in God's order during that episode in the Bahamas. However, God used what occurred there to teach a much needed lesson, not only for myself but for the body of Christ: *God is calling His Church to order.*

The Holy Spirit had warned me, "Learn the lesson well. Be sure that you listen. You don't know it all. Don't jump ahead of Me because if you do, you will make a fool of yourself." Moving in the strength of my own intellect, I had moved ahead of the Holy Spirit. When we move in the sufficiency of our own reason and intellect, there is an imbalance. Whenever the mind jumps ahead of the spirit, there is disorder. Where disorder prevails, there is an impending breakdown.

The body of Christ is experiencing such a breakdown. I believe that God allowed me to go through my breakdown in order to teach me His divine principle of order. Then I, in turn, would be able to communicate this invaluable lesson to the body of Christ so that we all might experience victory in this area. It is absolutely imperative that we have ears to hear what the Spirit of the Lord is saying and then obey Him. The Spirit of the Lord is higher than the mind of man. The mind is to be in subordination to the Spirit. Hear ye the word of the Lord: order!

It is difficult to explain what occurred in the Bahamas to the natural man. For those operating in reason and logic alone, it appears foolish. For those whose minds are spiritual, however, God is revealing a wealth of invaluable truth. Later, I repented to the people who were there because I was out of order. I had allowed my mind to direct my spirit against God's principle of order. The imbalance I was experiencing was a direct result of my mind directing my spirit. God led me into the wilderness of my mind because I was out of order and this imbalance needed to be rectified. God allowed me to go through this experience to humble me for the task of walking in His divine order. It is something that I pray will keep me humble the rest of my days.

CLINICAL DEPRESSION

Christian psychologists Dr. Frank Minrith and Dr. Paul Meyer state in their book, *Happiness Is a Choice*, that there are three major reasons for clinical depression, which was the ultimate medical diagnosis for my breakdown. The reasons are a lack of self-worth, a lack of intimacy with others, and a lack of intimacy with God.

The devil had been assailing me with questions that brought my level of self-worth down. He'd asked me, "What kind of leader are you? You make all these mistakes, but you say God is leading you? You don't have a spiritual mind or spiritual ears or spiritual eyes. You used to, but you don't now."

Then I had to come to terms with my lack of intimacy with others. I've always been a loner, preferring to stay by myself because of lifelong shyness. I've been bold and comfortable before large crowds, but uncomfortable one-on-one.

I also lacked intimacy with God. Specifically, I began to depend on my own reasoning with regard to an investment corporation we were involved with instead of relying on God's knowledge. I began to worry. I put mind over spirit. Disorder erupted in me and began to explode around me.

Among the symptoms of clinical depression are serious mood swings, unreasonable guilt; physical symptoms such as sleep disorders, overeating or undereating; anxiety, and irritability. The most serious symptom of clinical depression is delusional thinking, which occurs in very severe cases.

The delusional thinker is clearly out of touch with reality. They hear and see things that just aren't there. Very often the delusional thinker will become extremely suspicious and paranoid, believing everyone is out to get them.

According to the doctors, I reached the level of delusional thinking. I was seeing things that were not actually there. I was hearing and perceiving things that no one else was perceiving. I believed that people were out to destroy me, so I acted in mistrust, suspicion, and fear.

Doctors say that many who go through this kind of experience become permanently psychotic. I believe that it was only because I was born again and spiritually knowledgeable that the experience of my breakdown was different. Under the guidance of the Holy Spirit, I was able to clearly see many of the things I was going through. God forewarned me that if I allowed my mind to get ahead of my spirit, on those occasions I would lose touch with reality. Although I would make errors in judgment sometimes, ultimately I committed the keeping of my mind to God. I believe He kept me in His grace, which allowed me to learn from the mistakes I made without suffering irreparable damage to my psyche.

I AM KEPT

When Satan attacks, it is impossible to handle him in our own power. Our defense is the Word of God. The

Word of God is our source of victory against the onslaught of the enemy.

For the word of God is quick, and powerful, and sharper than any twoedged sword, piercing even to the dividing asunder of soul and spirit, and of the joints and marrow, and is a discerner of the thoughts and intents of the heart.

Hebrews 4:12

Because of God's Word, in spite of my disobedience and shortcomings, and through all the times I leaned to my own understanding, the Lord kept me in His grace and cleansed me with His blood. My confidence and my trust were in His strength and not my own ability.

There were times when I wasn't absolutely clear about everything. Separating illusion from reality became difficult. The confusion in my mind often clouded my ability to think clearly. One thing was certain, however: God was able to keep me from falling.

Now unto him that is able to keep you from falling, and to present you faultless before the presence of his glory with exceeding joy,

To the only wise God our Saviour, be glory and majesty, dominion and power, both now and ever. Amen.

Jude 24-25

SEPARATING ILLUSION FROM REALITY BECAME DIFFICULT. THE CONFUSION IN MY MIND OFTEN CLOUDED MY ABILITY TO THINK CLEARLY. ONE THING WAS CERTAIN, HOWEVER: GOD WAS ABLE TO KEEP ME FROM FALLING.

The scriptural promise of God's ability to keep me from being utterly destroyed stayed with me. I clung to the Word of God.

> **Behold, the eyes of the Lord God are upon the sinful kingdom, and I will destroy it from off the face of the earth; saving that I will not utterly destroy the house of Jacob, saith the Lord.**
>
> **Amos 9:8**

My complete trust was in God's faithfulness to His Word to uphold me and deliver me in the midst of my struggle with my sin. He kept me from falling, and He's going to continue to keep me from falling. He will present me faultless before the presence of His coming with exceeding joy.

> **For the which cause I also suffer these things: nevertheless I am not ashamed: for I know whom I have believed, and am persuaded that he is able to keep that which I have committed unto him against that day.**
>
> **2 Timothy 1:12**

I was suffering, but I knew in whom I believed and I knew that He was able to keep that which I had committed unto Him. All during this time, I prayed, "I've committed my mind to You, Father. I'm going through the wilderness of my mind, but I know You'll keep my mind. Dear God, my mind is Yours. I commit it to You." I thank God that He kept my mind against the day of my testing.

What I love about God is that if you ask Him to keep your mind, He keeps all of it. Here's an illustration that brings out this point more clearly. I have a watch. If I ask someone to take care of my watch, to keep it safe and give it back to me later, I expect just that. But suppose the person I allowed to keep the watch breaks it. He takes the crystal off, breaks the hands, and utterly defaces the watch. When he returns the bits and pieces of the broken watch to me, I'd say, "I asked you to keep my watch. Why didn't you keep my watch?"

His reply might be, "I did keep your watch, and I'm returning it to you."

It is clear that this person and I have two entirely different concepts of what it means to keep something. His concept of keeping my watch meant to just hold onto it, not giving attention to taking care of it. But I meant for him to keep my watch as a whole unit, intact, with the capacity to continue functioning upon its return to me. In other words, "keep it" meant to care for it and protect it from danger.

That is what God does for us. Whatever we commit to Him, He protects and keeps intact. He doesn't allow our trials and tribulations to rip us apart, but He guards us during all the trials and testings we go through.

When I came out of my warfare, I didn't expect to be a shell, not really knowing where I was, because I asked God to keep my mind. Therefore I was not surprised when the doctors gave me the report that my brain scan indicated no brain damage. I'd asked God to keep my mind, and He kept it without damage. God will keep you in perfect peace if you keep your mind on Him.

> **Thou wilt keep him in perfect peace, whose mind is stayed on thee: because he trusteth in thee.**
>
> **Isaiah 26:3**

While I wandered in the wilderness of my mind, God continually brought back to my remembrance a song my father used to sing. This song was an unlimited source of strength for me, as it spoke powerfully of God's Holy Ghost power to keep us alive. I knew Jesus was literally keeping me alive.

INCURABLE 1 PERCENT

Drs. Minrith and Meyer say, "Every human will suffer temporary grief reaction from time to time, but if a person puts into practice the knowledge he gains, there is no reason why he should ever get clinically depressed, unless he has a genetic bipolar disorder which occurs in only one percent of the population. For the other 99 percent, happiness in the long run will be his choice."

Happiness is a choice. For many years I was in the 99 percent who had no problem. Happiness was my choice. But in the hospital, I was diagnosed as being part of the one percent who has this bipolar disorder, and well-respected doctors said there was no cure. My doctor explained to me how serious this disorder is and how many people it afflicts. He told me that with the aid of doctors and medicine, they would be able to control it. But I realized the battle was not medical.

I was fighting a battle that I knew was spiritual. I knew the devil had not led me there and that it was a Matthew 4:1 experience. The Spirit of the Lord led me into the wilderness to be tempted by the devil.

> **Finally, my brethren, be strong in the Lord, and in the power of his might.**
>
> **Put on the whole armour of God, that ye may be able to stand against the wiles of the devil.**
>
> **For we wrestle not against flesh and blood, but against principalities, against powers, against the rulers of darkness of this world, against spiritual wickedness in high places.**

Wherefore take unto you the whole armour of God, that ye may be able to withstand in the evil day, and having done all, to stand.

Ephesians 6:10-13

I believe that I was in the unknown realm for a purpose. In this realm, I was out of my mind and disobedient to God. It was unlike the earthly realm where I obeyed Him. In this unknown realm, I would not listen to His voice because I was Paul Morton, the preacher, the pastor, the bishop. I knew the Bible, but in this realm, "the letter killeth, but the Spirit giveth life."

I needed to listen to the Spirit. Self had to die. It had to be Him and not me. In this realm, I died. The Spirit of the Lord literally took me through the process and broke me down, so He could break me up and break me out. I had to do spiritual warfare and I wasn't ready in the unknown realm. In order to prepare myself for spiritual warfare, I had to go through a spiritual fight.

While I was in this unknown realm, the doctors said my bipolar disorder couldn't be healed, because it was passed down through my genes. Well, I had a problem with that information. First of all, I was taught that there is no disorder in God. There is no breakdown. That was my first problem. Secondly, if there is a disorder and you turn it over to Him, He can bring it back into order.

Although the doctors were saying, "No cure, so accept it and live with it," I said no!

> **But though we, or an angel from heaven, preach any other gospel unto you than that which we have preached unto you, let him be accursed.**
>
> **Galatians 1:8**

The Bible says that even if an angel comes preaching something contrary to God's Word, we shouldn't accept it. Therefore, even if a noted psychiatrist comes preaching something contrary to His Word, we shouldn't accept it.

Under their conventional wisdom, the doctors assured me that my depression and anxiety could stay balanced with medicine. They prescribed Depakote, an antidepressant, to bring me up and Zypreza to bring me down. The cost of these medications was about $300 per refill. They said it was important for me to stay balanced. If I became depressed, I might commit suicide, or the disorder could go the other way and my strong, gifted side could cause me to go mad. They insisted that the medicine would balance me.

So I could choose to have the $300 prescription filled and refilled forever, or be balanced in Jesus. I decided that I would let Jesus balance me. I walked out of the doctor's office and said to my wife, "I cannot take this medicine. God has healed me." Now please understand that I'm not

THE BIBLE SAYS THAT EVEN IF AN ANGEL COMES PREACHING SOMETHING CONTRARY TO GOD'S WORD, WE SHOULDN'T ACCEPT IT. THEREFORE, EVEN IF A NOTED PSYCHIATRIST COMES PREACHING SOMETHING CONTRARY TO HIS WORD, WE SHOULDN'T ACCEPT IT.

suggesting anyone else should do what I did! This was what the Spirit was saying to me, and me alone. *This is not for everybody.*

This was right for me, however, because I had been assigned to do warfare and I had to be balanced in the Spirit. Jesus balanced me through spiritual warfare, not medicine. He stopped me from leaning too much to the right or too much to the left. I didn't have to worry about a genetic bipolar disorder because God had said, "I will keep you in perfect peace when your mind is stayed on Me." (See Isaiah 26:3.) I knew God's order would heal my depression and anxiety.

THE FLESH IS WEAK

As we fight our spiritual battles, we always have to remember that we're still in fragile bodies that have needs. Even when we fast to keep a sharp spiritual edge, we have to use discernment to keep from overstressing the temple of the Holy Spirit to the point that our senses become dulled as a result of denying our body its normal intake of fuel. Satan came to Jesus when his body was weak from hunger and his natural senses were dulled.

In my period of testing, I had been on a fast for approximately twenty-one days. During the fast, however, I was running on the treadmill every morning for over an hour, working my body at an accelerated speed. Even worse, there were times during the fast when I would restrict myself from drinking water. My body was dehydrated. I was expending much more energy than I was replenishing back into my body, which is a sure formula for imbalance and disorder.

God's order is that the Holy Spirit ministers to our spirit man, our spirit man ministers truth to our minds, and then our renewed minds minister life to our natural bodies. That's God's order. If God's order is going to work in us, we must realize we're in natural bodies. We're to keep our bodies under submission, but we shouldn't abuse them to the point of collapse, which is what I did.

One of my central problems was my schedule. With all the things I was doing, I was behaving like someone with a supernatural body, which we don't get until we get to heaven. The one we have now is mortal and requires care. We are to nurture and care for the natural body God has given us until we go to heaven. The Holy Spirit within us and the judgment and experience of our renewed mind will say, "Stop body! You're overdoing it!" If we overuse and abuse our bodies, that is disobedience. We are out of order.

That's a lesson God had to teach me the hard way, and because of my experience, I exhort all leaders in ministry to take time out and rest their bodies. God is calling us to bring our trinity — spirit, mind, and body — into order. We're busy doing the Lord's business, but we are not resting. It is important that we as Christians learn to stop, be still, and rest our bodies. We must learn to spend time relaxing and renewing our strength. There is a time to be Mary and a time to be Martha. It's part of God's order for us to balance rest and work.

So many of my fellow leaders and preachers cannot remember the last time they went on vacation. Let me encourage you to take one! Your church will be fine without you for a little while. If your ministry is to truly benefit from you, it needs all of you. If you are fatigued and exhausted, you are not able to truly impart or deposit into your church. Please hear me, men and women of God, there is a grave price to pay for not resting. I've seen it in myself, in other pastors, and in my own family.

My daddy was a workaholic. He was always doing the Lord's work. My mother was the one who kept us balanced. Dad was spiritual, but Mom kept us down to earth. I was the seventh child out of nine children, born when my father was 54 years old. My mother was 23 years younger than he was.

My dad possessed a great sense of humor, but he was usually a very serious man. He was my hero. I would sit on the first row in church every Sunday and watch closely as he preached. I wanted to be like my dad. It didn't bother me that he didn't do many of the things that other fathers did, because I understood he was a man of God and he had to attend to the things of God, not me. I realized how important he was to the body of Christ.

At a young age I saw my father, through the power of God, open blind eyes, unstop deaf ears, and cause those who were lame to walk. Watching my father flow in the power of God was absolutely amazing. He was a remarkable man. I can recall many nights when I was unable to sleep. I would come to the downstairs area of our home, and at 3 a.m. it was not an uncommon thing to see my father sitting in his special chair praying and reading the Word of God. He was an incredibly spiritual man, and I loved him tremendously.

Dad died when I was twelve years old, and there was a great void in my life. Although my dad was gone, I knew I was like him. I believed that the Holy Spirit was with me the way He was with my dad. I had his God-consciousness. There was no way I could have remembered all of the messages my dad preached, many of the illustrations he used, or the songs he sang, unless the same Spirit who had rested upon him now rested upon me.

It has recently occurred to me that many of the things that I've implemented in my own ministry are parallel to things in my father's ministry. I was born in Windsor, Ontario, Canada, where my father pastored a church. My father concurrently served as pastor of a church just across the border in Detroit, Michigan. My father's church was not just one church in two locations, it was one church in two countries.

Each Sunday my father traveled between our church in the United States and our church in Canada via the Ambassador Bridge or the tunnel. Each location had separate Sunday morning services, but on Sunday nights both congregations came together, alternating between locations. Ministering to two congregations in three services made for an exhausting Sunday.

Like my hard-working father, I minister to three congregations. Responding to the needs in our community, Greater St. Stephen expanded to one church in two locations. If you have something that's good spiritually, a church that is changing a generation, you should grow and produce your kind as in Genesis 1:24. Expanding our church to two locations, and ultimately three locations, is a concept that in hindsight I realize was a spiritual legacy inherited from my father.

Founding churches is a generational blessing inherited from my father, and I'm not the only one who has received it. My oldest brother, Bishop C. L. Morton Jr., now pastors Mt. Zion, where my father once ministered. The sons of Mount Zion were placed in different cities: Harrow, Chatham, Buxton, and Amesburg in Ontario; and Pontiac and Flint in Michigan.

I inherited my dad's good side, but I also inherited his bad side. With so much on his plate, so many demands on his time, Dad never relaxed. In my breakdown, I realized that not only did my heritage contain generational blessings, but the workaholic tendency I inherited was a generational curse. Generational blessings are wonderful, but it is imperative we recognize and break generational curses.

I realized that I was just like my daddy — work, work, work. No time to relax. I was always doing the Lord's work. I was failing to realize that a portion of the Lord's work was for me to take care of my body, because it is impossible for me to work all the time. Taking time to relax and having fun with family is part of the life and calling God has given me as well. My children understood their daddy was busy and had a lot on him. I thank God I have not neglected my family, though I've worked extremely hard, but I have determined to be a better husband, a better father, and a better friend.

Thank God I differed from my father in that I realized I could choose. I had to choose to either continue abusing my body and busying myself with the Lord's work right into an early grave, or stop and minister to my total man. I chose to minister to my total man. My father died at 65 years of age, but the doctors said that he died with the body of a 90-year-old man. His body was worn out. He was an awesome man of God, a great father, and he is still my hero, but he did not minister to his total man.

This was an invaluable lesson for me. I refuse to put my ten-year-old daughter through the trauma of losing her father this early in her life simply because I'm not ministering to my entire being. God has called us into order.

The only thing that restrained Jesus on earth was His body. His body got tired and He rested. Perhaps that's why He said, "Greater things shall ye do." (See John 14:12.) We understand that our God-consciousness is not greater than Jesus' was, nor is our self-consciousness as great as Jesus'. But in body He knew that we would be able to do more than He was able to do because of the times in which we would live. He knew that we'd be able to catch a plane and fly around the world to minister the Gospel, and that we'd be on television to minister to millions at a time.

Nevertheless, we must be just like Jesus when it comes to physically resting our bodies. We must know when to stop. If we don't, it will result in a breakdown, a heart attack, or a stroke. Our bodies will let us know that we're out of order!

If the Holy Spirit says you need medical help, then by all means see your doctor. If He tells you to fast and pray and put your body under for a couple of days, then set aside some time when you don't have to focus on anything but Him and His Word. When you obey the Spirit, you are in order. The Holy Sprit does not want you to die before your time, before you have lived the full and successful life God has planned for you.

In all areas of your life, don't ever allow your mind to tell you something contrary to the Holy Spirit or the Word of God. Don't listen to your mind. Don't listen to the lies, enticements, and deceptions of the enemy. Listen to the Spirit and take God at His Word. That's the key to maintaining God's order in every area of your life.

Chapter 5

The Devil's Tactics

But I fear, lest by any means, as the serpent beguiled Eve through his subtilty, so your minds should be corrupted from the simplicity that is in Christ.

2 Corinthians 11:3

The devil's ultimate goal in the life of a Christian is to make sure our thinking prevails over God's voice. When he achieves that, he renders us ineffective in the work of the kingdom. In the realm of spiritual warfare, we become wounded soldiers barely hanging onto life. We must defeat the devil's efforts to take us out of the battle, and to do that, we must learn his subtle tactics and weapons. The devil always comes against Christians with three weapons — temptation, accusation, and deception — but he often uses them in subtle ways that can fool even the mature Christian.

Temptation

Through temptation, the devil appeals to our lust of the flesh. He knows what we like, what feels good to us —

and it's not just sex. He knows we're tempted to gain power, influence, money, position, attention, and so forth by any means available. And Satan also knows from experience to hit us in our soft spots. If we love money, for example, he will tempt us to steal and cheat to get it. If we have a tendency to lie, he will always put us in a position where it's profitable and easy to lie. And the subtle angle that Satan puts on temptation is that he hits us where we think we're strong, because he knows we're weak.

One of Satan's favorite subtle temptations is to cast doubt on the Word of God. Two prime examples of this trick are his encounters with Eve and with Jesus. In each case, he misinterpreted the scriptures to tempt. In the third chapter of Genesis, he tempted Eve by casting doubt upon the words God had spoken to Adam. "Eve, what did God say?" he asked. After she repeated what God had said to Adam, Satan said to her, in essence, "Eve, that's not true. God just doesn't want you to have your eyes opened to good and evil."

We must be mindful of this trick. Eve had received God's Word secondhand from Adam, and when she told Satan what God's instructions were, she added a little of her own opinion. Satan knew he had her on shaky ground. Not only must we thoroughly study the Bible for ourselves to know exactly what God said, but we also must guard against Satan's constant attempts to cast doubt on that Word and cause us to get out of order.

When Jesus was led by the Holy Spirit into the wilderness, Satan tried to twist the meaning of Scripture to tempt Him. (See Luke 4:1-13.) He said to Jesus, "If You're *really* the Son of God...." Although Satan knew perfectly well that Jesus was the Son of God, he wanted to get Jesus to sin by misusing His power and disobeying His own Word. So Satan said, "I won't believe You're the Son of God until I see You turn these stones into bread or jump from the pinnacle of the temple."

Satan knows the Word of God, so he will come at us in the same way he came to Eve and Jesus, attempting to trick us into doubting or changing the Word. He knows that if we truly know, believe, and stand on the Word of God, we will have the victory over him every time he tangles with us.

For instance, the Word says, **For all have sinned, and come short of the glory of God** (Romans 3:23). But Satan will twist the meaning of that scripture to tell us everybody's sinning, including us, so we're bound to come short of the glory of God in every instance. He wants us to make it an excuse to give in to temptation. While it's true that all have sinned and come short of the glory of God, it's not true that everybody is living a life of sin and we might as well join them. This scripture is given to teach us that no one person can look down on another as if they were better, because all have sinned. We all are living under grace.

In the face of Satan's temptations, we must seek to be dead to sin. Do dead men lie? Do dead women commit adultery? Dead people don't respond to temptation at all. Although we're new creatures in Christ, we still have to fight temptations. As long as we're in our earthly body with its sin nature, the old man will keep coming alive. We have to resist temptation and kill him every day. If we let him stay active and undisturbed by resistance, he'll grow quickly and take over. The old sinful nature fights against our spiritual man, and if we fail to resist, it causes us to become weaker and weaker. Eventually our love for God and His people lessens.

To resist the temptations that appeal so much to our old sinful nature, the apostle Paul said, "I die daily." (See 1 Corinthians 15:31.) He said he voluntarily killed his flesh and submitted to the Spirit of God every day. To successfully resist temptation and thereby continue to respond to the voice of God, we too must kill the old man every day.

> **Likewise reckon ye also yourselves to be dead indeed unto sin but alive unto God through Jesus Christ our Lord.**

Let not sin therefore reign in your mortal body, that ye should obey it in the lusts thereof.

Neither yield ye your members as instruments of unrighteousness unto sin: but yield yourselves unto God, as those that are alive from the dead, and your members as instruments of righteousness unto God.

Romans 6:11-13

I am crucified with Christ: nevertheless I live; yet not I, but Christ liveth in me: and the life which I now live in the flesh I live by the faith of the Son of God, who loved me, and gave himself for me.

Galatians 2:20

I'm dead to sin, and dead folks don't respond to temptation. How do I know I'm dead? Because I choose to conform my life to this scripture, which tells me I'm dead to sin but alive unto God through Jesus Christ. It's no longer "I" who live, but Christ who lives in me. I'm alive only through Jesus Christ.

While going through my breakdown, the devil used deception by twisting the Word of God. With my wife and doctor, I would get very quiet, refusing to talk and becoming a loner. The voice behind the curtain was saying,

"Keep doing that. You're just like Jesus. Don't respond." Jesus stood silent before those who condemned Him.

> **He was oppressed, and he was afflicted, yet he opened not his mouth: he is brought as a lamb to the slaughter, and as a sheep before her shearers is dumb, so he openeth not his mouth.**
>
> **Isaiah 53:7**

The doctor tried to give me medicine. I was quiet. He and Debra would call out my name, and I could hear them, but I wouldn't answer. The voice behind the curtain would tell me I was like the lamb brought to the slaughter. The only way I would come out of this unknown realm was through the Word of God. I would hear the people of God praying for me or singing a praise song, and somehow the real voice of God would break through all the deception and I would recognize His voice. Even though my mind was messed up, the Word that had been hidden in my heart over the years would bring me back to reality.

I can see now how people can go into a state of shock and never talk again. It is because the devil can play powerful tricks with the mind. You see, the devil knows the Scriptures. That's why you have to watch him and fight him with the rightly-divided Word.

EVEN THOUGH MY MIND WAS MESSED UP, THE WORD THAT HAD BEEN HIDDEN IN MY HEART OVER THE YEARS WOULD BRING ME BACK TO REALITY.

> **Study to shew thyself approved unto God, a workman that needeth not to be ashamed, rightly dividing the word of truth.**
>
> **2 Timothy 2:15**

Under the influence of this spirit of deception, I was not worried about my reputation in the unknown realm. The voice behind the curtain told me to be like Jesus, and He was never worried about His reputation. The devil knew my concern about my reputation, and he tried to turn the situation to his benefit. The spirit of deception was strong. It made me believe I was just like Jesus, but I was out of fellowship with Him because of this wall of deception. The spirit of deception spoke the Word and said,

> **But made himself of no reputation, and took upon him the form of a servant, and was made in the likeness of men.**
>
> **Philippians 2:7**

Jesus had laid aside His might, His power, and His glory by taking the disguise of a servant and becoming a man. He humbled Himself even further by actually dying a criminal's death on a cross. The cross was the symbol of shame, and a person's breakdown is a symbol of shame in our society. Therefore, I thought I was like Jesus now. Before, I was a man who guarded his reputation all the time, but now I didn't care anymore. I was like Jesus.

In the beginning, I would not go to the hospital, but now I was saying, "Take me through the front door." Those who took me were trying to be discreet, trying to keep me quiet, protect me, and take me through the back door. But I kept saying, "Take me through the front door. Don't try to slip me in the back because I'm Bishop Paul Morton." The devil was tricking me again. Thinking I was being humble, I really just didn't care. I didn't care how I looked or who saw me. I was not wise.

Still, through it all God was teaching me important lessons. Even though the spirit of deception was strong, I knew God was telling me something. I remember crying in the hospital, saying, "Lord, I surrender all to You. I'm confused, but I know what I'm going through is for a reason and whatever it is, You will work it out for my good."

> **And we know that all things work together for good to them that love God, to them who are the called according to his purpose.**
>
> **Romans 8:28**

The devil meant it for evil, but God meant it for good.

ACCUSATION

Other subtle weapons the devil uses against Christians, especially those who are serving in the kingdom, are accusations that appeal to our pride. He will detect subtle forms of pride in us and then tell us the brethren are not appreciating us, are mistreating us, or are blind to our gifts. These sneaky accusations are especially effective among those who are called to ministry. It's a favorite trick of the devil to let you become puffed up only to tear you down. I know this trick all too well, since I've seen it in my ministry.

First Timothy 3:6 makes reference to how being a novice in a ministry can cause one to be lifted up in pride and easily fall into the condemnation of the devil. When we send people out to preach or put them in positions of authority too soon, we open them up for these prideful accusations. The body of Christ uses training and experience as insurance against this kind of pride.

Look at it this way: If someone wakes up one morning and says they want to be a brain surgeon, we don't just buy them a scalpel and send them to cutting. They must go and prepare themselves. Whether you are a plumber or a lawyer, an engineer or a teacher, you need training before you actually begin practicing in your field. But when somebody wakes up in the morning and says, "I'm called to preach," many times they're out preaching in a few weeks when they should be praying about Bible school and where they can serve in their church.

"God wants me to preach now!"

No, He wants you to prepare yourself first.

To prevent the spirit of pride from rising up and to counteract the accusations of the devil, our ministry or church requires anyone called to the ministry to take what we call the "Pride Test." After announcing their calling, they must immediately begin to prepare themselves. First, they must attend Sunday school for one year, where they listen to a teacher, interpret the lessons, and put them in sermon form. That helps them to zero in on exactly what they feel God wants them to do.

The second year, they get a few opportunities to teach. Having an audience helps them develop their public speaking ability. The third year is what we call "One-Year Prep" — one year of serious preparation for ministry. If someone doesn't want to go through the training, they can't be a part of our ministerial alliance. It's important that they learn that ministry is about serving with humility.

When novice preachers get out there and preach too quickly, they can easily get lifted up with pride and start saying things like, "I'm so good I ought to be preaching more." Then the devil whispers in their ears, accusing people of overlooking them or being jealous of their great talent.

But it's not just newly-called preachers who are targeted. Even when preachers go through the appropriate training and take the time needed to prepare properly, eventually the devil hits them with pride. It's a very human frailty. Folks line up to tell them how great their last sermon was, and after awhile the preacher forgets that it wasn't them who preached so well but the Holy Spirit in them. It's hard for them to remain humble when a thousand people hang onto every word they speak. It's hard for them to remember that they're just servants of the most high God like everyone in their congregation.

DECEPTION

Once accusation and pride take root in a Christian's life, a subtle form of deception can follow.

> **For I say, through the grace given unto me, to every man that is among you, not to think of himself more highly than he ought to think; but to think soberly, according as God hath dealt to every man the measure of faith.**
>
> **Romans 12:3**

Once we receive from God the grace and anointing that we need to minister, we must be careful not to be deceived in another way. It can happen so easily, especially if we have never felt good about ourselves or have never had very much. Before we know it, we forget that the anointing we've been ministering under is from

God, not from us. We forget that whatever gift we have been operating in, He merely loaned to us. We get a little proud. We may even get proud of our own humility!

God uses humble people, but the devil uses proud people. When we are deceived with pride, Satan gets the glory rather than God. To counteract our tendency toward pride, we should constantly keep the Word of God before us and give God all the glory. That is so important!

Romans 12:3 says that it is through grace that we are not to think more highly of ourselves than we ought. Through faith in God's Word, we transform our minds. We begin to think positively about ourselves and believe for all the great things God has given to us. Nevertheless, we understand that because God's grace is *unmerited* favor, we cannot take any of the credit. By renewing our minds in the Word, we realize that it's not us. It's Him in us.

God has dealt with us according to our faith. But where is our faith? Is our faith in ourselves, in our own abilities? Our faith must remain only in God, and that humble faith should cause us to allow the Holy Spirit to lead us at all times.

> **This I say then, Walk in the Spirit, and ye shall not fulfill the lust of the flesh.**
>
> **Galatians 5:16**

OUR FAITH MUST REMAIN ONLY IN GOD, AND THAT HUMBLE FAITH SHOULD CAUSE US TO ALLOW THE HOLY SPIRIT TO LEAD US AT ALL TIMES.

When we fail to walk in the Spirit and begin to have faith in our own wisdom, we set ourselves up to be fooled by the deceiver. He's waiting for opportunities just like that to lead us astray. If we don't want the devil to deceive us, we must realize our own wisdom will just get us into trouble. We need God's wisdom. So where do we get it?

> **If any of you lack wisdom, let him ask of God, that giveth to all men liberally, and upbraideth not; and it shall be given him.**
>
> **James 1:5**

God will give us the wisdom we need, and we must not limit our need for God's wisdom to the big questions of life. Making seemingly small decisions in our own wisdom will steer us off course just as surely as doing so in large decisions. If we don't get God's wisdom every day, the devil is sure to deceive us.

By the same token, we can't take pride in our own authority. I can't do anything spiritually in the name of Paul Morton or in the title of Pastor or Presiding Bishop. Nothing bows at the mention of my name. But God gives His authority to believers. We have all been given the name of Jesus. When we use the name of Jesus as if it were a Power of Attorney, we act in the authority of that name and get the same results that Jesus enjoyed during His ministry.

To operate in God's power, we must open our mouths and speak the Word of God with God-given authority. The sword of the Spirit is God's Word, spoken in faith by our mouths. We must aggressively resist Satan and drive him away with the power of God's Word from our mouths. Satan will wear us down if we allow him to hang around.

The devil fooled me with that spirit of deception. My fellowship with God was hindered, so the spirit of deception was able to step in and confuse me. Was it the Holy Spirit's voice or the spirit of deception? I knew that the only thing that could bring me out of my confusion was the Word. I knew God was not the author of confusion, so I knew something was wrong there. The very fact that there *was* confusion showed me that I was listening to the wrong spirit. If I hadn't had the Word in my heart, I would have stayed confused. Satan cannot fool you if you seek God through His Word. But you must know His Word.

Because of my experience with deception, I now fear for aggressive preachers. Doors are opening for them to boldly go out and preach the Gospel without being hindered by a lack of funds, but the spirit of deception is very strong. Some of these preachers have begun to want financial guarantees to preach or to demand 50 percent of the offering. They're being led by the spirit of deception!

Don't misunderstand me — I'm not talking about folks who are led to give an offering to a ministry. I'm talking about ministers who demand certain things that are not pleasing in God's sight, those who put their demands in the form of a contract. If the media got hold of their contracts, their ministries would end tomorrow. It would be a rebuke to the body of Christ.

Okay, we know the devil is a deceiver, but how do we keep him from deceiving us?

> **And be not conformed to this world: but be ye transformed by the renewing of your mind, that ye may prove what is that good, and acceptable, and perfect, will of God.**
>
> **Romans 12:2**

The *renewing of your mind* really indicates inward renewal and transformation by God's Word. We can't simply read a bunch of books or get a degree and think our minds have been renewed. Often the things we read don't touch our real problem. They only speak to our minds and not to our spirits. However, the transformation spoken of in Romans takes place only when we allow the Word of God to dig deep down within us. When we deal with our inward man first, the outward manifestations will follow.

The renewing of one's mind is essential to the Christian life. We find the perfect example of how crucial it is to renew the mind in my fellow African-Americans. African-Americans could be much further ahead in society if we didn't have a serious problem in our minds with anger for the white man. We still blame him for the injustice shown towards our race in the past. Our internal anger continues to hinder us from moving forward. Slavery is long over, yet we are still saying we will not improve ourselves until the white man pays us back. We think he owes us. We're believing man's wisdom and not renewing our minds with God's Word.

What has happened is that our anger has turned into excuses, and God hates excuses. You remember Matthew 25:14-30, where Jesus told the parable of the talents that a businessman distributed to his stewards. The servants were entrusted with the management of his estate. When the servant who was given the fewest talents made an excuse for why he didn't increase it, Jesus took the talent away. He gave it to the servant who had been given more initially and who was also most productive. The parable shows that if we're faithful in the little things, we'll be blessed with greater responsibilities and greater rewards. When we're tight-fisted with what little we have, we can't be trusted to deal properly with real wealth.

Despite this clear teaching from the Word, many African-American Christians still have a problem giving money to worthy causes. Even spiritual leaders who regularly ask their congregations to give have a problem with giving themselves. When we're asked to support a ministry, I've noticed we don't do as we should. Why? Because no matter how much of God's Word we receive and *say* we believe, far too many of us only see a black man and not a man of God. We think, "He only wants to take my money and get over on me."

This inward mistrust for each other stems from unrenewed minds. Our minds have not yet been renewed, even though we say we're spiritual and we say we've been changed. Until we have a renewal of the mind from the Word, this attitude toward money and white people will continue to show up in our lives. We're still being deceived.

You see, in that old state, we can't see what God wants. God wants us to give our money to bless others, yet we can't get past our mental distrust. I pray that the curse of mind over spirit in that area will be broken and that African-Americans will trust God and take Him at His Word.

Look at it this way: In the natural, we don't open our doors to strangers because we don't trust them. So when we don't open the door of our hearts for God, it indicates that we don't trust Him. When African-Americans don't trust Him, it's because we don't trust one another, and that's because we don't like ourselves. We don't like ourselves because that old deceptive image is still in our minds and in our spirits. We don't like the image we see: the slave in chains, the poor man standing in welfare lines, the *Amos & Andy* character portrayed as dumb and ugly.

We must break that spirit of deception and be transformed by the renewing of our minds. We must go inside and see why we still have that image of ourselves. We must be transformed until we like who we are. If we don't allow this renovation to take place in our minds, things will remain the same year after year. We must be careful that our minds do not become minds of the flesh, which can never see what God sees. We thank God for the new point of view He gives to us in His Word.

When we die daily to the temptations of sin, when we humble ourselves to avoid pride, and when we keep our minds transformed by the Word of God, we avoid becoming wounded soldiers in spiritual warfare. With faith in God's Word and in the power of the name of Jesus, we defeat the devil's efforts to take us out of the battle. God's voice prevails over our thinking and we walk in God's order.

Chapter 6

WHAT HAPPENS AFTER?

The Bible says in Luke, chapter 4, that Jesus was led by the Holy Spirit into the wilderness to be tempted by the devil. When the forty days of temptation and testing were finished, there was something different about Jesus. Consider the following passage of Scripture:

> **And Jesus returned in the power of the Spirit into Galilee: and there went out a fame of him through all the region round about.**
>
> **And he taught in their synagogues, being glorified of all.**
>
> **And he came to Nazareth, where he had been brought up: and, as his custom was, he went into the synagogue on the sabbath day, and stood up for to read.**
>
> **And there was delivered unto him the book of the prophet Esaias. And when he had opened the book, he found the place where it was written,**

The Spirit of the Lord is upon me, because he hath anointed me to preach the gospel to the poor; he hath sent me to heal the broken-hearted, to preach deliverance to the captives, and recovering of sight to the blind, to set at liberty them that are bruised,

To preach the acceptable year of the Lord.

And he closed the book, and he gave it again to the minister, and sat down. And the eyes of all them that were in the synagogue were fastened on him.

And he began to say unto them, This day is this scripture fulfilled in your ears.

Luke 4:14-21

After a wilderness experience, it would seem that you would be tattered and worn from the constant warfare between spirit and mind. You would think that a season of resisting the tugs and hits of the devil, all the while running into the arms of God, would leave anyone ready for a rest and a vacation. But to the contrary, once the tests have been passed, the lessons have been learned, and direction has been given, there is a compelling urge to go to work. Jesus did exactly that after His wilderness experience, and so did I.

Although I was only in the hospital for a week, it seemed like an eternity. When the day came for Debra to pick me up, she was there bright and early, because I had expressed to her on the phone that my desire was to leave as soon as possible. Once I was told I was "good to go," leaving was all I could think about! However, as the weekend passed by slowly and I awaited my departure, leaving became less and less desirable. I found myself sad to leave behind those whom had been my peers, those who were still struggling with their mental and emotional well-being. Ministry began to call, and I could not leave them without a word of deliverance, comfort, and freedom.

Some knew Jesus and some didn't. For those who did, I begin to minister to them that Jesus was their deliverer, His Word was the sword with which they were to fight, and that life and death were in the power of the tongue. (See Proverbs 18:21.) To those who didn't know Jesus, I recommended Him! Overwhelming compassion came over me as I prepared to leave on that Monday. Some whom I had ministered to earlier that week had calmed down, but there were others who were continuing to fight despair and depression or were filled with rage and anxiety. I began to lay my hands on each one of them as I said good-bye. One of them smiled and told me she was glad I had come there and that she would watch me on television. My wife stood by in amazement, for it was only a few days ago that she had seen me in a similar state. I was not amazed. It was my ministry!

As I walked out of the hospital that day, the words rang in my ear, "Glad you came!" It's so like the Lord to send us "through" only for us to come out saying, "Glad I went through!" It's all about purpose and destiny. It so mirrors the life of Jesus. After each great period of testing, He came out with great victory and purpose in ministry. Furthermore, Jesus never came out and left the scene before empowering others. The man in the graveyard, once full of demons, was now at His feet. Jesus told him to go and save his household. (See Mark 5:1-20.) To the woman at the well, He said, "God is a spirit, and you must worship Him in spirit and in truth," and she brought many in Samaria to Jesus. (See John 4:7-30.) To the disciples He said, "As I was sent, I am now sending you." He laid His hands upon them and said, "Receive ye the Holy Ghost." (See Mark 3:14-15 and John 20:21-23.)

My test, my breakdown, proved no different. It was to get me ready and focused for the next great move of God, in the closing moments of this century and into the next millennium. Since the week I spent in the hospital, my ministry has intensified in the area of winning the lost and destroying the works of the devil. I have begun "Crescent City Fire" crusades across this country, which are doing just that. Many people from all walks of life are being delivered as I do what God has called me to do. My wife (whom God showed me would work with me) and I are on a mission, determined to obey God until He says to stop. Signs and wonders are already being manifested as we share with them our experience during my breakdown. On the road many are being saved and delivered as a result of our testimony.

Today, seeing souls saved is the most important mission of the Church. The wealth of the wicked is laid up for the people of God to get the job done, to win the world to Jesus, so we must stay focused. We must constantly seek and save that which is lost. If we are in the body of Christ, then we must continue to carry on Jesus' ministry in Jesus' order. We must seek the kingdom and His righteousness first, then everything we need and desire will be supplied. (See Matthew 6:33.)

What happens after deliverance? We are empowered with a renewed sense of purpose and an overwhelming passion to see people come to know Jesus and be set free as we were. Furthermore, we want them to avoid the sin and error we fell into and thus escape the terrible consequences. Then, after we get others saved, healed, delivered, and set free, we send them out to do the works of Jesus also. That's what the second part of this book is all about: staying out of trouble if you're not in it, and getting out and continuing to stay out if you are in trouble.

WHAT HAPPENS AFTER DELIVERANCE? WE ARE EMPOWERED WITH A RENEWED SENSE OF PURPOSE AND AN OVERWHELMING PASSION TO SEE PEOPLE COME TO KNOW JESUS AND BE SET FREE AS WE WERE.

PART TWO:

THE KEYS TO RESTORING AND MAINTAINING GOD'S ORDER IN THE KINGDOM

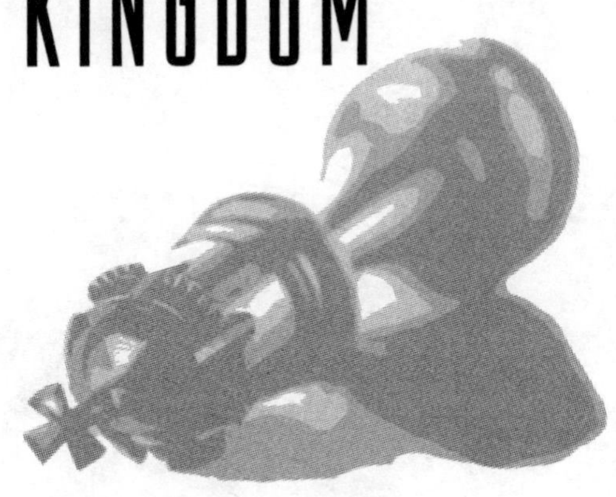

Chapter 7

THE BRIDGE BETWEEN TRADITIONS

While many of you are being blessed by this book, some of you are sitting there with your teeth grinding, thinking, *I thought this guy said he was Baptist! What's he doing talking about tongues and the discerning of spirits? We Baptists know that stuff went away with the apostles! What gives?*

The gap between my Pentecostal roots and my Baptist roots are at the very core of my story, so it's important that we explore these differences and how we can bridge the gap by the Word of God. Part of my healing and restoration came when I realized that these two traditions and ways of viewing the Gospel, in opposition to each other, were tearing me apart. In the end, to be healed I had to take the truth of God's Word which resided in each tradition and become whole through the Word and only the Word.

My doctor says *I* have a genetic bipolar disorder, but *the body of Christ* has a spiritual genetic bipolar disorder between Fundamentalists and Pentecostals. Based on the

Word of God, our fellowship of churches, the Full Gospel Baptist Church Fellowship, is simply taking the best of both worlds to the glory of God. We are seeing how this is breaking down walls that have divided us for decades and bringing healing to the body of Christ.

BAPTIST VS. PENTECOSTAL

On the spiritual side, the good side, I love the Baptist church for its structure. Their foundation is solid, because their foundation is salvation in Jesus Christ. Some Pentecostals want to jump right over salvation and a relationship with the Lord Jesus Christ. All they want to know is if you've been filled with the Holy Ghost and speak in tongues, overlooking the fact that we can't be filled with the Holy Spirit until we've met Jesus. Yet Baptists are so hardheaded about the application of the Holy Spirit, they can't see what they lack.

I love the Pentecostal freedom in worship and Pentecostal faith. In Pentecost, we feel free to praise Lord in the Spirit with exuberant jubilation. We allow the joy we feel to come out in our worship. How can you sing about the blood of Jesus without getting excited? I also love the way Pentecostals believe the Word by faith, while many Baptists have to reason everything out, trying to decide with their own wisdom whether the God who still saves also still heals.

Since my roots are in both Pentecost and in the Baptist tradition, I found myself right in the middle. I was torn between two traditions, neither of which *exactly* squared with the Word of God. On my Pentecostal side, I felt that every time I sinned, every time I came short of the glory of God, I had to get saved all over again. On the Baptist side, I had a good scriptural foundation but was told we didn't believe in speaking in tongues or that anything in the second chapter of Acts had application today. Baptists believed in the cross and the blood of Jesus, things necessary for a good foundation, but never understood spiritual warfare. They believed most of the Word, but they didn't go far enough.

So I was in a tug-of-war between my roots in the Pentecostal church and my place in the Baptist church and loving both. But there were some things in my life that I had to break up in order to break out. I had to break down and allow God to break up my spiritual genetic disorder.

I believe that I was literally experiencing generational curses on the Baptist and Pentecostal sides. To get in God's order, I had to stop listening to dead tradition of preachers, teachers, and doctrines. I had to go to the source and see the bridge between the two sides, which is

TO GET IN GOD'S ORDER, I HAD TO STOP LISTENING TO DEAD TRADITION OF PREACHERS, TEACHERS, AND DOCTRINES. I HAD TO GO TO THE SOURCE AND SEE THE BRIDGE BETWEEN THE TWO SIDES, WHICH IS THE TRUE WORD OF GOD.

the true Word of God. The only thing that can bring Baptist and Pentecostals together is His Word. It took my experience to see the bridge clearly.

There are too many genetic disorders in the body. We need to give each other a break, to open our hearts to each other. After all, Baptists are being filled with the Holy Ghost every day, yet some self-righteous Pentecostals still don't believe that Baptists are even saved. Break the generational curse! Bind that self-righteous spirit! The Word clearly states, "I will pour out My Spirit on *all* flesh." Yea, verily, even unto First Baptist deacons!

On the other hand, there are still some Baptists who think all this Pentecostal power is crazy. Tradition just won't allow them to believe in being filled with the Holy Ghost, manifesting the gifts of the Spirit, the power to speak in other tongues, and the manifestation of supernatural spiritual power. It is time to break that Baptist generational curse. Command that curse to be gone in the name of Jesus! Bridge the gap with the Word of God.

THE INFILLING

Here's how I see the infilling of the Holy Spirit: When I was saved, I was baptized in Jesus. The infilling of His Spirit, the fullness of His Spirit, comes with stirring up the gift of the Holy Spirit. I want the Holy

Spirit to take full control of my life until I have power over the enemy, power over demons, power over my finances, power over sickness, and power to live right. Stir up the gift, and Jesus will fill you up.

What a lot of Baptists don't know yet is that you can't stay up on all God has called you to be and do just with your mind. When we're praying to God, we want to understand it with our natural minds. But the Bible says that the Holy Spirit may speak a heavenly language through us, so that we don't know exactly what we're praying. And Baptists need to understand that it's okay — there are things your mind doesn't know or doesn't need to know.

> **In the same way, the Spirit helps us in our weakness. We do not know what we ought to pray for, but the Spirit himself intercedes for us with groans that words cannot express.**
>
> **And he who searches our hearts knows the mind of the Spirit, because the Spirit intercedes for the saints in accordance with God's will.**
>
> **Romans 8:26-27 NIV**

When I pray in the Spirit, I don't know what to say. The Holy Spirit speaks through me, and Jesus takes the prayer to the Father. I pray even when I don't know what to pray for. This is not natural. This is spiritual. We allow spirit to rule over mind and our heavenly language to express what the Holy Spirit is praying.

We have a choice of weapons in spiritual warfare. Our mind or His mind. Our tongue or His tongue. Our language or His language. Who's in charge? But don't get the order of the Holy Spirit wrong. Remember that the power to live right or the fruit of the Spirit comes first, then the gift of speaking in tongues.

Again, God's Word does not lie. It is written that God will pour out His Spirit upon all flesh and our sons and daughters shall prophesy. (See Joel 2:28.) If we attribute the manifestations of the Holy Spirit to the devil, we're treading on very dangerous ground. We must overcome dead tradition with the Word of God. By the power of the Word of God, we break the curse and bridge the gap between the Pentecostal and Baptist.

ONCE SAVED...

My foundation in the Pentecostal church told me that if a Christian sinned, they had to be saved all over again, but that's not the Word. That's dead tradition. During my experience in the wilderness, I was mixed up in my thoughts, listening to the wrong voice because of my disobedience. I broke off my fellowship with God. I think I embarrassed Him. I was His preacher, but I'd been deceived by Satan. Through it all, however, God never let me go.

During this time of trial I learned that these words of Jesus are still true:

> **My sheep hear my voice, and I know them, and they follow me:**
>
> **And I give unto them eternal life; and they shall never perish, neither shall any man pluck them out of my hand.**
>
> **My Father, which gave them me, is greater than all; and no man is able to pluck them out of my Father's hand.**
>
> **And I and my Father are one.**
>
> **John 10:27-30**

No one can snatch me out of His hand! I didn't know where I was or what I was doing, but I did know I was God's child and I didn't want Satan. The devil offered me power and glory, but I wanted only Jesus. No matter what the devil tempted me with, he could not pluck me out of the Father's hand.

If we are believers, the enemy cannot pluck us out of God's hands. Baptists believe that once you're saved, you're always saved. So will everyone in our churches make it to heaven? Well, allow me to make this distinction: I believe

IF WE ALLOW GOD'S WORD TO SHOW US HIS ORDER, AND WE ALLOW GOD'S ORDER TO PREVAIL OVER OUR WAYS, OUR OLD MAN MUST BREAK UP AND DIE BECAUSE THE NEW CREATION IS BREAKING OUT.

everyone who is truly saved will stay saved, *but many folks we think are saved in reality aren't.* They certainly act as if they are believers. They look like believers, they sing like believers, and they pray like believers, but they're not **because strait is the gate, and narrow is the way, which leadeth unto life, and few there be that find it** (Matthew 7:14).

How can we tell the difference? A true believer knows Jesus intimately and understands that the Holy Spirit is real. No matter how angry they get at God, a real believer never blasphemes the Holy Ghost. It's acceptable to be angry or to get upset, but do not curse the Holy Ghost because it is the one and only unforgivable sin. I didn't say it, Jesus said it:

> **I tell you the truth, all the sins and blasphemies of men will be forgiven them.**
>
> **But whoever blasphemes against the Holy Spirit will never be forgiven; he is guilty of an eternal sin.**
>
> **Mark 3:28-29 NIV**

I believe that we can tell those who have the appearance of being Christians but have never really been saved by how they deal with and speak of the Holy Spirit. It's very sad to know that some folks are just impostors, pretending to be in the body of Christ.

THE POWER OF GOD'S WORD

This generational curse, with its denominational traditions, extends into all areas of Christian life and ministry. If you refuse to believe that God has called women into ministry, for instance, you have a problem with choosing tradition over the Word. Break that curse with the Word. Let it go! If you believe that God only uses certain styles of music, that hymns are holy and praise choruses aren't, you're putting tradition over the Spirit. Break the curse!

Within the Church, we also have to break the power of family problems brought on by other generational curses. Many are dealing with hate because of molestation, incest, and other abuses. Or perhaps your father ran out on you and left you to be raised by a single mother. As a result, you are mad at the world. As bad as those things are, it's even worse to be wrapped up in hate and anger so tightly that you can't have a relationship with the living God! Break that curse right now! Forgive those who sinned against you, then ask God to deliver you from the generational curse and bring your disorder into order.

In the same way, God can heal other disorders. He can heal my depression. If I'm too low, He can bring me up. If I'm too high, He can bring me down. He is the healer of all my anxiety, guilt, and pain, because I've renewed my mind with the solid fact that **there is therefore now no condemnation to them which are in Christ Jesus, who walk not after the flesh, but after the Spirit** (Romans 8:1). I don't wallow in my feelings, I revel in the truth of God's Word!

Often we are confused about what to do in our lives and our pride prevents us from seeking help. Consequently, we get a helpless, hopeless attitude toward life and just go with whatever seems easiest or least painful. To relieve our confusion and hopelessness, we need to renew our minds by the Word of God and get godly guidance to know what to do. The Word of God promises that God is interested in directing our lives if we let Him.

> **In all thy ways acknowledge him, and he shall direct thy paths.**
>
> **Proverbs 3:6**

> **The steps of a good man are ordered by the Lord: and he delighteth in his way.**
>
> **Psalm 37:23**

> **Order my steps in thy word: and let not any iniquity have dominion over me.**
>
> **Psalm 119:133**

If we allow God's Word to show us His order, and we allow God's order to prevail over our ways, our old man must break up and die because the new creation is breaking out. God is saying to the Church that order is His way. If we strive to walk in Him, He will be with us through the tears and pain. He'll be right there to keep us in perfect peace. It is because of Him that we can have joy and happiness. Jesus is our balance. We have the power of the Holy Spirit and we are persuaded that neither death nor life, nor demon powers, nor the devil's principalities, nor things present nor things to come, will separate us from the love of God. (See Romans 8:38.)

God desires that we get our spiritual lives in order and not allow man's traditions to prevail over His Word in our lives. You don't have to be a Baptist or a Pentecostal to know certain truths. Truth is not a Baptist thing. It's not a Pentecostal thing, or a Church of God in Christ thing. God's Word is truth.

The bridge between traditions is the Word. If we are going to get in order, renew our minds, and break generational curses, it will be achieved through our individual and corporate submission to the Word of God.

CHAPTER 8

SPEAK THE WORD ONLY

The centurion answered and said, Lord, I am not worthy that thou shouldest come under my roof: but speak the word only, and my servant shall be healed.

Matthew 8:8

I know we live in a new day now, but when I was growing up my parents' words were law. I rarely questioned what they told me, and I certainly never contradicted them. What they said, we did. By the same token, to stay in God's order we need to speak God's words and act on them. God's words must prevail over our words, just as God's Spirit must prevail over our minds.

Most people aren't aware of the power of the words they speak, but we truly have whatever we say. Every day we are confessing what we're going to get tomorrow. If we don't like what we had today or this year, we must change what we say. We must line up what we say with what God's Word says, and it will become true in our lives. We put our faith into action with our mouths.

The mouth of a righteous man is a well of life.

Proverbs 10:11

Death and life are in the power of the tongue.

Proverbs 18:21

If we are confessing the Word of God, we are speaking life into our lives and into others. If, on the other hand, we are constantly confessing the reality of our terrible circumstances, we are speaking death into our lives and into those around us. Negative words and negative thoughts become self-fulfilling prophecies.

For verily I say unto you, That whosoever shall say unto this mountain, Be thou removed, and be thou cast into the sea; and shall not doubt in his heart, but shall believe that those things which he saith shall come to pass; he shall have whatsoever he saith.

Therefore I say unto you, What things soever ye desire, when ye pray, believe that ye receive them, and ye shall have them.

Mark 11:23-24

Do you know what Jesus is saying? "You already saw Me do miracles, and you believe I can heal people, but when I leave it's going to be up to you. You must speak to the mountain in My name. Don't expect Me to move it. I expect *you* to move the mountain *in My name.*"

This is another area where tradition goes against the Word. I can hear God saying, "People are not talking to the mountain as I told them to. They are just talking to Me."

We say, "Lord, I know You can do it. I know You can move this mountain."

But Jesus is saying, "Stop, hear what the Spirit of the Lord is saying. You are not talking to your mountain. You are just talking to Me. The Word of God says, 'Whatever *you say* to the mountain will happen.'"

Are you just saying, "Oh, Jesus, I pray You'll heal my headache"?

When is the last time that you had a conversation with a headache? "Hey headache, you're coming out! You will not have any authority in my head! You have me in pain, but I have the authority over you in the name of Jesus. Head, I command that you line up with the Word of God and be healed!"

Look at how Peter and John healed the lame beggar at the Beautiful Gate in Acts 3:6. The lame man was looking at them for a handout, but they gave him a hand up. Peter said,

DO YOU KNOW WHAT JESUS IS SAYING? "YOU ALREADY SAW ME DO MIRACLES, AND YOU BELIEVE I CAN HEAL PEOPLE, BUT WHEN I LEAVE IT'S GOING TO BE UP TO YOU. YOU MUST SPEAK TO THE MOUNTAIN IN MY NAME. DON'T EXPECT ME TO MOVE IT. I EXPECT YOU TO MOVE THE MOUNTAIN IN MY NAME."

Silver and gold have I none; but such as I have give I thee: In the name of Jesus Christ of Nazareth rise up and walk.

Notice that Peter didn't pray, "Oh Jesus, heal this man." He knew that they had been given authority by God to use Jesus' name directly. They told the man to rise in Jesus' name. Their words had supernatural, spiritual power because they lined up with His Word.

So then faith cometh by hearing, and hearing by the word of God.

Romans 10:17

Many of us pray for the sick according to tradition, without effect, and soon lose our faith in healing. We must go back to the Word and line up our words accordingly, because the Word of God produces faith, and the Bible says that where the Word of the King is, there is power! (See Ecclesiastes 8:4.)

CAT GOT YOUR TONGUE?

To speak words that line up with God's Word, we must talk with words coming out of our mouths — not just thinking it, but speaking it. As a dad, I often know what my children want without their asking, but I want them to ask and communicate their needs and desires to me. At times they may say, "Oh, Daddy! You know what

I'm talking about!" However, my response is, "No, you tell me."

Jesus directs us to speak out loud, not thinking thoughts with our minds, but saying words with our mouths. This has the additional effect of showing our faith and the power of our words to others. Look at the story of Jesus raising Lazarus from the dead in John 11. Jesus raised Lazarus with the words, "Lazarus, come forth," but prior to that He spoke to God out loud so that others could hear:

> **And Jesus lifted up his eyes, and said, Father, I thank thee that thou hast heard me.**
>
> **And I knew that thou hearest me always: but because of the people which stand by I said it, that they may believe that thou hast sent me.**
>
> **John 11:41-42**

James 1:22 says we should be doers of the Word, not just hearers. We must do what we've heard, and we must not waver in our faith after we've spoken the Word.

Look again at Mark 11:23: We speak to the mountain in the name of Jesus, but we must not doubt in our hearts, and only *if we believe that those things which we say shall come to pass, shall we have whatever we say.* In other words, saying the words without faith, or with wavering faith, won't do anything.

But let him ask in faith, nothing wavering. For he that wavereth is like a wave of the sea driven with the wind and tossed.

For let not that man think that he shall receive any thing of the Lord.

For a double minded man is unstable in all his ways.

James 1:6-8

You have to say to cancer, "You can't stay in my body, cancer. In the name of Jesus, you can't kill me!" You have to say with your mouth, "I will not die with cancer," and keep saying it and believing it. When the doctor comes with a negative report, you can say, "Okay, doc, that's your opinion and I appreciate it, but I know that by His stripes I'm healed and sickness has to go in the name of Jesus." Then don't go around telling everybody what the doctor said, confirming it with your mouth. Go tell everybody what the Word says, and don't waver.

This doesn't just apply in the area of healing. Whatever the mountain is in our lives, we must tell it to go in the name of Jesus.

That at the name of Jesus every knee should bow, of things in heaven, and things in earth, and things under the earth.

Philippians 2:10

THIS IS NOT THE GAME "SIMON SAYS." I DON'T MERELY REPEAT WHATEVER GOD'S WORD SAYS LIKE A MINDLESS PARROT. NO, I MUST BELIEVE GOD. I MUST ABSOLUTELY BELIEVE THAT WHAT HE SAYS TO ME IS TRUE. THEN AND ONLY THEN WILL IT COME TO PASS.

Everything must bow the knee at the name of Jesus. When we have financial problems, we begin talking to our money. We can tell our checkbooks to line up with God's Word. We can command our cash flow to come under the government of God's Word. If we're giving our last dollar in an offering, we must speak to that mountain of lack. We must say as Dr. Leroy Thompson would say, "Money cometh to me." If we plant money in faith, we expect money to return to us. We're not crazy. If we plant beans then we expect to harvest a crop of beans. It's a solid biblical principle of sowing and reaping, planting and harvesting. The principle is applicable that when you give money to God, money cometh to you.

Again, all of this is predicated on one thing — solid, unwavering faith.

> **And Jesus answering saith unto them, Have faith in God . . . believe that those things which he saith shall come to pass.**
>
> **Mark 11:22**

This is not the game "Simon Says." I don't merely repeat whatever God's Word says like a mindless parrot. No, I must believe God. I must absolutely believe that what He says to me is true. Then and only then will it come to pass.

What is going to happen if we speak God's Word out of our mouths with faith? Our mountains, whatever they are, will be cast into the sea. God's Word will prevail over our thinking, man's wisdom, and unbelief. Generational curses and the dead traditions of man will be overthrown. Because we believe God and take Him at His Word, God's order will overcome our disorder.

CHAPTER 9

TAKING AUTHORITY

For though we walk in the flesh, we do not war after the flesh:

For the weapons of our warfare are not carnal, but mighty through God to the pulling down of strong holds.

2 Corinthians 10:3-4

As I've said before, this is a spiritual battle we're waging. We can't successfully fight using our own thinking, our own traditions, or our own authority. Reading God's Word renews our minds and builds our faith, and speaking God's Word keeps us in His order. Then we also need to study the authority that has been delegated to us in His Word to deal with the spiritual forces of darkness around us.

For we wrestle not against flesh and blood, but against principalities, against powers, against the rulers of the darkness of this world, against spiritual wickedness in high places.

Ephesians 6:12

To deal with demonic principalities and satanic powers, we must understand how Jesus dealt with them. Let me first make one thing clear: *It is impossible for demons to possess a child of God,* but they can *oppress* us. They can confuse us, deceive us, lie to us, scare us, and make us believe things that aren't true. They can make our lives miserable, our Christian walk a painful stumble, and our testimony a pitiful complaint.

Most Christians would prefer to pretend there are no evil spirits and deny their effects, calling it bad luck or fate. That doesn't work. We can all remember when we were afraid of something as children. We would pretend that it wasn't there, hoping it would go away. But we cannot be immature when dealing with the kingdom of darkness.

Demons are real and they must be confronted in the authority of Jesus Christ. Demons have a great hand in destroying our society, our homes, our schools, and our jobs. They incite violence, lust, greed, and all destructive behaviors. People who do not know Jesus do not know what the root of these problems is, but believers know that their root is Satan and his demons.

Satan is doing all he can to thwart the plan of God, and he knows that his time is short. Therefore, we must boldly tear down the kingdom that Satan is trying to establish. We must reclaim our schools, our homes, and our society. But first of all, we must reclaim our own minds from the influence of the devil.

How did Jesus deal with these evil spirits, these demons? He used His God-given authority.

> **And they went into Capernaum; and straightway on the sabbath day he [Jesus] entered into the synagogue, and taught.**
>
> **And they were astonished at his doctrine: for he taught them as one that had authority, and not as the scribes.**
>
> **Mark 1:21-22**

They were amazed at the authority with which He taught the Word of God. Jesus taught with authority, not like their preachers, the scribes. There are a whole lot of people bringing the Word of God today, but they have no authority. When they preach, lives remain the same. There is no change, no deliverance. They offer platitudes and tickle ears with high-sounding words, but don't preach the Word with the authority that Jesus delegated to His Church.

So what did Jesus do with the authority He had?

> **And there was in their synagogue a man with an unclean spirit; and he cried out,**

Saying, Let us alone; what have we to do with thee, thou Jesus of Nazareth? art thou come to destroy us? I know thee who thou art, the Holy One of God.

And Jesus rebuked him, saying, Hold thy peace, and come out of him.

Mark 1:23-25

In their synagogue was a man with an unclean spirit, or a demon. Just as demons were real and manifested themselves in Jesus' day, they are real and manifest themselves today. We often find them in church, just as Jesus did.

Did you notice that the demon recognized exactly who Jesus was when nobody else did? Demons have known Jesus forever, and they don't like Him. When He comes on the scene, they know they are going to be destroyed. That's also why demons attack those of us who belong to Jesus. They hate us and the power we have in His name. They don't want to hear about Jesus, so they cry out, "Leave us alone. Don't mention Him in my house, leave us alone."

That's precisely why we are seeing so much trouble in our schools. The devil moved those with worldly authority to forbid prayer and Bible reading in the schools, and our world is suffering severely as a result. Listening to the evil spirits is destroying the very fiber of our young people. We have allowed demons to rest comfortably and work unchecked in institutions and areas that should be governed by the Church's authority. These demons have cried out for us to leave them alone and we have heeded their pleas.

Violence? "Leave us alone."

Abortion? "Leave us alone."

Adultery? "Leave us alone."

Spiritual counseling? "Leave us alone."

PRAY AND REPENT

As the Church of the living God, we must be careful to *not* leave these demons alone. We must utterly overthrow everything that is not in compliance with the Word of God and bring them into subjection to the authority of Jesus Christ.

> **The kingdom of heaven suffereth violence, and the violent take it by force.**
>
> **Matthew 11:12**

There's no doubt we need God to heal our land, and as Christians, we should be leading the effort to restore America. God's Word tells us how:

> **If my people, which are called by my name, shall humble themselves, and pray, and seek**

As the Church of the living God, we must be careful to NOT leave these demons alone. We must utterly overthrow everything that is not in compliance with the Word of God and bring them into subjection to the authority of Jesus Christ.

my face, and turn from their wicked ways; then will I hear from heaven, and will forgive their sin, and will heal their land.

2 Chronicles 7:14

God promises that if His people, people called by His name, would just humbly pray and seek His face, and repent and turn from their wicked ways, then He would hear from heaven and heal our land. He would clear our conscience and forgive our sins. God is saying that He has power to heal the land, disease, and corruption, but He will do it only if people who are calling themselves by His name will humbly pray and repent.

"But," I can hear God say, "you prefer fleshly things, carnal things, over those things that are spiritual. So instead of being humble, you are exalted in self. Instead of praying, you are playing. You're using your privilege of communication with the Father as a last resort only after you have tried to fix things yourselves and have failed."

The Church is not seeking the face of God. We seem to have too much on our own busy agendas to look and see what He wants us to see in Him. Therefore, if I exalt myself instead of praying and I play, seeking only those things I want instead of His face, then I will not turn from my evil ways. Our land will never be healed. It will be destroyed, and not because of the devil, but because *we didn't fight the devil.*

The devil is always going to do everything he can to gain access to our lives. He never gets tired of messing with us. When we disobey God's command to seek His face, we give Satan an open door to wreak all kinds of havoc in our lives. When we are disobedient to God's commands and do not pray and repent of our sin, we are opening a door for demonic oppression.

The choice is ours. Spirit over mind or mind over spirit. A healed land or a land riddled with infirmity and disease. Forgiven or unforgiven. God hearing us from heaven or God ignoring our voices. The choice belongs to us. When we see the blessings that come from choosing spiritual things versus the curses that come from choosing carnal things, our need to choose spiritual things becomes blatantly apparent.

Look at the rest of God's promise to those who humbly seek Him:

> **Now mine eyes shall be open, and mine ears attend unto the prayer that is made in this place.**
>
> **For now have I chosen and sanctified this house, that my name may be there for ever: and mine eyes and my heart shall be there perpetually.**
>
> **2 Chronicles 7:15-16**

God chose to tabernacle or abide with us, and if we're to work in His authority, it has to be our choice to abide with Him too. God could have put a mechanism in us to make us do His will like robots, but He wants our decisions to come from our will and our heart. He is not going to make our choice for us. He will show us good and bad, right and wrong, light and darkness, and we must make the choice.

Choose you this day whom ye will serve...but as for me and my house, we will serve the Lord.

Joshua 24:15

This is spiritual. Our house is our own lives. To be in God's order, we must hear what the Spirit of the Lord is saying. The Holy Spirit will speak to our spirit man, our God-consciousness. Our spirit man will speak to our mind, our self-consciousness, and our mind will speak to our body, our outward consciousness. Our houses will then be in order. As for me and my house, we will serve the Lord. We must each speak to our house and say, "House, get in order." If we get our spiritual houses in order, our natural houses will follow and get into order too.

CLEANING HOUSE

And Jesus rebuked him, saying, Hold thy peace, and come out of him.

Mark 1:25

Jesus rebuked the demon. He told the demon to be quiet. Whenever a demon is oppressing us, confusing us, talking to us, deceiving us, keeping us up with a sleeping disorder, keeping us sick with a physical disorder, we must tell that demon to be quiet and get out of our house.

"Be quiet!" we tell them. "I will not entertain you! I don't want to hear what you have to say because you're a liar and a deceiver. I command you in the name of Jesus, be quiet. Be quiet and get out. Go immediately! You kept me up for the last night, you got my stomach in knots for the last time. Go! You will never make me fearful again. Go!" We must not play with demons. In Jesus' name, tell them to be quiet and go!

And when the unclean spirit had torn him, and cried with a loud voice, he came out of him.

Mark 1:26

Because some spirits are more powerful than others, some demons are going to fight more than others. They're going to resist coming out. But Jesus gave us His authority. If we have to wrestle awhile, it's okay. Sometimes it will take prayer and fasting to build our faith, as Jesus spoke of in Matthew 17:21. We know one thing: One way or another that demon is coming out!

And they were all amazed, insomuch that they questioned among themselves, saying,

> **What thing is this? what new doctrine is this? for with authority commandeth he even the unclean spirits, and they do obey him.**
>
> **Mark 1:27**

Wouldn't you like people to see you minister and ask, "What new thing is this?" The new level that God is taking us to now is deep spiritual warfare. People are going to be amazed when we manifest the authority Jesus had. But too many of us say, "Oh, but that was Jesus! I'm just little old me!" That's dead tradition talking. That's the old man. We have authority — if we're willing to use it in faith.

Jesus said that He gave us the keys to the kingdom.

> **And I will give unto thee the keys of the kingdom of heaven: and whatsoever thou shalt bind on earth shall be bound in heaven: and whatsoever thou shalt loose on earth shall be loosed in heaven.**
>
> **Matthew 16:19**

These keys of authority represent power. Jesus said, "I am returning to heaven, but I am going to leave you fully equipped. I am giving you these keys now for spiritual warfare." Religious tradition says, "Oh yaasss, we'll have the keys to the kingdom once we get to heaven." No! It is

IF WE HAVE TO WRESTLE AWHILE, IT'S OKAY. SOMETIMES IT WILL TAKE PRAYER AND FASTING TO BUILD OUR FAITH, AS JESUS SPOKE OF IN MATTHEW 17:21. WE KNOW ONE THING: ONE WAY OR ANOTHER THAT DEMON IS COMING OUT!

important that we use the keys *now* because when we get to heaven we'll no longer need them. There are no demons in heaven!

We need to use the keys to the kingdom *now*. When Jesus said He'd give us the keys of the kingdom, He was giving us the power of heaven to use now. We must learn what kind of power we have as Christians in the here and now, because the battle is going on now. The mind is warring against the spirit now. The devil is seeking whom he may devour now.

The Bible says we are destroyed because of a lack of knowledge. (See Hosea 4:6.) We often do not possess enough knowledge of the Word of God to understand the power available to us now. Jesus gave to us to use today the same power and authority He had when He walked the earth. We must accept the fact that whatever we bind on earth shall be bound in heaven and whatever we loose on earth shall be loosed in heaven. We can stop things or make things happen.

Now the whole point of cleaning our house of demonic power and taking authority in Jesus' name is to walk in the divine order of God. If we abide in Him and His Word abides in us, we can ask whatever we will in His name and He will give it to us. (See John 15:7.) That's good news! We can literally render the attacks of the enemy null and void. We have the power to stop the devil from attacking physically, mentally, and spiritually. When we believe this with our hearts and speak it with our mouths, we deploy all of God's power against the enemy.

MATURITY

Walking in God's authority to clean house requires a certain level of spiritual maturity, of course. Not everyone is responsible enough to use these keys wisely. All three of my children are true, bonafide Mortons, but they didn't get keys to our home when they were young children because of their immaturity and their carelessness. My wife and I could not entrust everything in our house to their care when they were babies. In their immature state they could have misused or misplaced their keys, leaving our house vulnerable. Only when we saw each of our children being responsible in other areas of their lives could we trust them with keys to our home.

Our heavenly Father deals with us in the same manner. Through various trials and tests, God watches to see how responsible we are with the knowledge and power He has given to us. Will we misuse it for our own purposes? Will we give Him the glory? Will we allow His Word and His will to abide in us so that He will be in control of the things we desire of Him?

When God sees that we can be trusted with His power, He then gives us the keys to His power to use with whatever we are dealing with on the earth. We reach a higher level of power as we reach a higher level of responsibility. Irresponsibly misusing the power in the name of Jesus is dangerous when dealing with demonic powers. Look at the story of the seven sons of Sceva in Acts 19:

> **Then certain of the vagabond Jews, exorcists, took upon them to call over them which had evil spirits the name of the Lord Jesus, saying, We adjure you by Jesus whom Paul preacheth.**
>
> **And there were seven sons of one Sceva, a Jew, and chief of the priests, which did so.**
>
> **And the evil spirit answered and said, Jesus I know, and Paul I know; but who are ye?**
>
> **And then the man in whom the evil spirit was leaped on them, and overcame them, and prevailed against them, so that they fled out of that house naked and wounded.**
>
> **Acts 19:13-16**

The devil has to obey Jesus, and he has to obey anyone who bears His name in faith. However, if someone just tries to use the power as a parlor trick or for personal gain, they just may find themselves buck-naked and bleeding! The sons of Sceva did not serve God; they served themselves. They used God's power for their own gain. A mature believer is a believer who has completely surrendered their life to God and all they say and do is to His glory alone.

I've found that praise and worship are vital tools to focus my spirit on the things of God and away from things of the flesh. We are encouraged in Psalm 100 to enter into His gates with thanksgiving and enter into His courts with praise. Praising God gets me into the throne room of God and more of God into my heart and life.

Praising God is a key to focusing God's power on our situations, because the spirit is willing, but the flesh is often weak. When difficult situations arise in our lives, our fleshly inclination may be to complain. But if we choose to praise God instead, knowing by faith in His Word that we have everything we need, our spirit will rule over our flesh.

THE OLDEST LIE – AND REMEDY

Now the serpent was more subtil than any beast of the field which the Lord God had made. And he said unto the woman, Yea, hath God said....

Genesis 3:1

We must remember that we are dealing with a cunning enemy who's refined his tricks over centuries. Satan will try to make us believe that our keys won't work. "Hath God said?" God says they will work, but Satan comes with his lies declaring that they won't work. The moment we waver, the moment we say, "Well, maybe this time they won't work," Satan has made us doubt God's Word. And the moment we doubt God's Word, we lose the key. The key opens the door. If we lose our key by doubt, by allowing our mind to rule over our spirit, we're not going to be able to get the door open.

The devil searches high and low for our lost keys. If we lose our keys to him by doubt or allow him to convince us that they aren't important, then we lose our ability to bind and loose. Satan will then bind us. Our ministry and testimony will be damaged, and we are out of God's order.

When that happens, we rarely will admit the problem and repent. We just go on. Imagine the hypocrisy needed to save face when God has given us the power to bind and loose in His name, but we've allowed Satan to derail us. Then we're the ones who are bound and unable to get loose. The devil will have us behaving totally opposite to what the power of God would allow us to reign in.

Satan desires glory and power. He will do his best to undermine the power God has given us, to pervert us in some way. Then he can wield power over us and prevent us from bringing glory to the King of Glory. But even if he is successful in doing this, the oldest lie also has the oldest remedy: repentance and cleansing through the blood of Jesus. Let us never be too proud to admit our sin, whether it is doubting God's Word or committing adultery, repent, and allow God to cleanse us from all unrighteousness. Because when we do that, God restores us to the place of authority and we again hold the keys to the kingdom.

Chapter 10
OUR HEALER

You may have gone through or are going through some of the same things I went through. You may have experienced some level of defeat. So it is crucial that you understand that Jesus is with you and that He is your Healer — the Great Physician, the Balm of Gilead — and He heals you and restores you in every area of your life: spiritually, mentally, emotionally, physically, financially, and socially; in your family, in your profession, in your church, in your community, and in your nation.

> **For an angel went down at a certain season into the pool, and troubled the water: whosoever then first after the troubling of the water stepped in was made whole of whatsoever disease he had.**
>
> **And a certain man was there, which had an infirmity thirty and eight years.**
>
> **When Jesus saw him lie, and knew he had been now a long time in that case, he saith unto him, Wilt thou be made whole?**

The impotent man answered him, Sir, I have no man, when the water is troubled, to put me into the pool: but while I am coming, another steppeth down before me.

Jesus saith unto him, Rise, take up thy bed, and walk.

And immediately the man was made whole, and took up his bed, and walked: and on the same day was the sabbath.

John 5:4-9

I see our world in this situation. Our world is sick, gathered around a pool, just waiting for something to happen. Some are waiting for luck. Some are waiting for chance. Some are waiting for an inheritance. I've decided I'm waiting on Jesus.

Our lives are not based on luck. Our lives are not based on chance. As righteous believers, our steps are ordered by the Lord. We do what the Holy Spirit and God's Word say. We walk as God wants us to walk, and we talk as He wants us to talk. He has a plan for our lives. He is walking with us through every situation in our lives, asking, "Do you want to get well? All you have to do is say 'yes.'"

If you are sick in your body, sick in your mind, or disturbed in your spirit, tell the Lord, "I want to get well."

Don't try to argue with Him in the flesh. Jesus asked the lame man a question: "Will you be made whole?"

Instead of saying, "Yes!" he just made excuses. He said there was nobody to put him into the pool. In 38 years, nobody ever put him in the pool when the angel troubled the waters. But Jesus said, "I didn't ask you that. Do you want to get well?" If we don't have that desire, it won't happen.

"Yes, I want to get well, but somebody always steps in before me." There are some things we must do to help ourselves. It would seem to me that sometime in that 38 years he could have tried to help himself. He could have practiced rolling his body directly into the pool. He could have done something to get into the pool. Jesus is not going to do everything. We're going to have to help ourselves. So often we want everybody else to help us, but what are we doing to help ourselves?

The old folks used to say, "If you take one step, He'll take two." God is ready to deliver us. We don't need to wait on a pastor or some traveling evangelist we've seen on television. Jesus is here. This world is sick but thank God, Jesus is here. This man had lost hope, but Jesus came through asking, "Will you be made whole?"

Focusing on our circumstances, doctors' opinions, and our own tradition, we forget the power that is in

Jesus' hand. "But Lord, I have been stumbling here for 38 years, *I can't* walk." Those two words — *I can't* — will keep us from claiming victory in our lives. Don't confess doubt from your mind, confess faith from the Word:

> **I can do all things through Christ which strengtheneth me.**
>
> **Philippians 4:13**

I could hear the man saying, "Let's be realistic here. I've been trying for 456 months to get into the pool. That's 1,976 weeks, 13,870 days, and I haven't made it yet."

But Jesus said, "I'm not worried about that. Rise, take up your bed, and walk." The man was so busy looking at the water, he almost missed Jesus.

God's thoughts are not our thoughts. His ways are not our ways. We cannot expect God to jump through our little hoops, thinking He's going to work the most logical way, the most obvious way, or the traditional way. He works the way He wants to work. Since we don't know exactly how the Lord is going to work, we just have to listen when He speaks and respond to His voice.

A BALM FOR HEALING

> **Behold the voice of the cry of the daughter of my people because of them that dwell in a far country: Is not the Lord in Zion? is not her**

DON'T CONFESS DOUBT
FROM YOUR MIND,
CONFESS FAITH
FROM THE WORD.

king in her? Why have they provoked me to anger with their graven images, and with strange vanities?

The harvest is past, the summer is ended, and we are not saved.

For the hurt of the daughter of my people am I hurt; I am black; astonishment hath taken hold on me.

Is there no balm in Gilead; is there no physician there? why then is not the health of the daughter of my people recovered?

Jeremiah 8:19-22

When Jeremiah asked the questions, "Is there no balm in Gilead? Is there no physician there? Why then is not the health of the daughter of my people recovered?" We feel his burden over the sin and destruction of God's people. Jeremiah, with his loyalty to God and his deep relationship with God, is concerned over those who are far away from God by their own choice. He is worried. "Is not the Lord in Zion? Is He not in the Church anymore? Where is God? Why have they provoked Him to anger?" The people had made graven images, building their own gods. They were involving themselves in things that were far from God.

"The harvest is past, the summer is ended, and we are not saved." How many people do you know who hear the Gospel but are not saved? They've heard the Word of God and they think they understand what God is all about, but they will not be saved. They give mental assent to the reality of God, but they have not given their hearts to Him. Because of this, Jeremiah is disturbed. In fact, Jeremiah is so hurt that he wants to leave the people forever.

> **Oh that I had in the wilderness a lodging place of wayfaring men; that I might leave my people, and go from them! for they be all adulterers, an assembly of treacherous men.**
>
> **Jeremiah 9:2**

It's terribly painful for a godly man to see people deliberately miss God. They're rebellious, they refuse to repent, and they refuse to change. It's so very disappointing when we have a heart for God and we yearn to see the will of God accomplished in someone's life, yet they remain unchanged. Is there no balm in Gilead? The unsaved people are Gilead. Is there no healing in them? Is there no way out for their lives? If their name is Joe, they are Joe Gilead. If their name is Mary, they're Mary Gilead. But thank God there is a balm in Gilead.

The balsam tree containing the balm is a little shrub, never growing past the height of three or four feet, and spreading like a vine. Its juice is used to make a medicinal balm. The Word of God is the balm made from the juice. The juice in this Word will heal you. Drink of His Word. There is healing — physical healing, mental healing, spiritual healing, whatever kind of healing you need in your life — available to you if you drink His Word.

We must seek and find the balm of Gilead. If we're really concerned about the balm for the healing of the nation, for the healing of our lives, we must seek and find it. But it's not easy. Gilead is the mountainous region east of the Jordan River which forms the frontier of the Holy Land. The name Gilead means "a hard rocky region." We find our healing in the hard and rocky region filled with mountains. We must go through a hard, rocky region, but if we endure, there is a healing to be found there.

The healing found in Gilead will not be found by the casual, unobservant traveler who happens to pass by. No, we must seek this blessing out. We must climb up the rocks that lead to Gilead. Scale the heights. Diligently search among the rocks for the precious storm-stunted shrubs that yield the healing medicine for our souls. No pain, no gain. No cross, no crown.

Drink of His Word. There is healing – physical healing, mental healing, spiritual healing, whatever kind of healing you need in your life – available to you if you drink His Word.

The balm in Gilead will not be found in religious idleness. There are too many people who don't want to do anything for God, and yet they expect to be blessed. They want to be healed so they can go back to watching those trashy television talk shows in comfort. They don't want to have to read the Word, pray, and seek God's face. But this is serious business. It requires an effort to press towards the mark, which involves exerting ourselves and continuing to work at it. We must press toward the mark and keep pressing.

HEARTS FOR GOD

We live in a diseased world. Man doesn't believe in God. We don't believe in His Word. Man is ignorant of truth. Ignorance comes from the word "ignore." We simply ignore God and ignore truth. If it doesn't fit into our agenda we ignore it. Consequently, we gradually move into a hardness of heart rather than a heart open to God's Word. Men harden their hearts against God and His Word because their hearts are not suited to deal with the truth inherent in God's Word.

> **The heart is deceitful above all things, and desperately wicked.**
>
> **Jeremiah 17:9**

As Christians, our problem is earthly-mindedness, a carnal mind that will not submit to the Spirit of God. This causes imbalance in a believer, because the Spirit is not in control. This is how the devil slips in and takes authority. Since we're proud, we still want people to think we're deeply spiritual, so we still come to church, we still pretend to praise God, but then when we go out we run with His enemy. We become hypocrites. We come to church as a formality, or because our grandmother taught us that if we don't come to church God will do something bad to us.

How many people do you know who hate spiritual duties? They don't want any responsibility. They just come to church, sit there, then leave, never realizing that God is reaching out with the balm of Gilead, their healing. In the flesh, we're trusting in our own righteousness. There is a balm in Gilead, but we have to reach for it. We have to stir ourselves up on the inside and turn our hearts to God.

When we turn our hearts to God, He will pour His healing balm on our lives.

JESUS KNOWS

Jeremiah goes on to say, "Is there no physician there?" With all this trouble, all these demons, all the depression, all the oppression that we see, is there no physician that can help us? Oh yes! Jesus is the Master Physician. Look at His credentials. He's our Creator and He knows what we need before we ask.

Many times our problems arise because we won't go to the doctor. How many times have we known there was something wrong in our physical bodies but kept putting it off because we didn't want to hear what the doctor had to say? But it is truth that sets us free. No longer can we continue to put things off and not deal with them because we feel better not knowing. We go to the truth, to Jesus, to deal with the problem.

Jesus knows all about us. All we have to do is go to Him and find out what He knows. He can see everything. Many have come to Him thinking they had a fatal disease. They thought that it was over. Naturally speaking, we may go to the doctor because of a chest pain. We immediately think, *Heart conditions run in my family, so something must be wrong with my heart.* Thank God for medical doctors who are able to see beyond what we feel and let us know what is actually occurring in our natural bodies.

But that's what Jesus does as well. He looks at our situation and says, "I can fix this. I can heal you." It doesn't matter that the devil has said, that we cannot get deliverance because of who we are and what we've been through. What matters is that Jesus is saying, "I can heal you."

There are those who come and think there's nothing wrong with them. They think that they're just fine. There are some killer diseases, such as hypertension, where there's no pain. A tumor can grow inside us and not cause pain until it's far advanced. The doctor, however, can let us know that there's something wrong.

In the same way, Dr. Jesus can also let us know when something is wrong — spiritually, mentally, emotionally, or physically — even though we may not yet detect it. So often we get wrapped up in busyness and pride and we think more highly of ourselves than we ought. We believe everything is fine when it is not. But God be thanked, Dr. Jesus knows how to bring us back to reality. Look at what He says to the church at Laodicea:

> **Because thou sayest, I am rich, and increased with goods, and have need of nothing; and knowest not that thou art wretched, and miserable, and poor, and blind, and naked:**
>
> **I counsel thee to buy of me gold tried in the fire, that thou mayest be rich; and white raiment, that thou mayest be clothed, and that the shame of thy nakedness do not appear; and anoint thine eyes with eyesalve, that thou mayest see.**

As many as I love, I rebuke and chasten: be zealous therefore, and repent.

Revelation 3:17-19

Jesus will let us know, "No, you are not 'all that.' You need to get into My Word and pray more."

Here is Dr. Jesus' prescription: Humble yourselves before God and wait on Him to receive all He has for you. Do all He tells you to do and all you know to do from His Word. Give your hearts completely to Him, and His blessings will flow into your lives.

Jesus always give us the right prescription!

Chapter 11

KNOWING HIM

I count all things but loss for the excellency of the knowledge of Christ Jesus my Lord: for whom I have suffered the loss of all things, and do count them but dung, that I may win Christ,

And be found in him, not having mine own righteousness, which is of the law, but that which is through the faith of Christ, the righteousness which is of God by faith:

That I may know him, and the power of his resurrection, and the fellowship of his sufferings, being made conformable unto his death.

Philippians 3:8-10

Throughout all my experiences, I have maintained a deep desire to really know Jesus. During my time in the wilderness, the Holy Spirit led me to deal with my guilt, my lack of self-worth, my lack of intimacy with others, and my lack of intimacy with Him. All of this came about because I wanted to know Him. I found that knowing

Jesus is a progressive experience. Paul talks about it in his letter to the church at Philippi.

What Paul desired was not just knowledge *about* Jesus. He wanted to know Him in a direct, immediate, and personal way. He did not want to know Him in the sense of intellectual apprehension, but in the sense of practical experience. There is a world of difference between knowing *about* a person and *knowing* a person. We know about people whom we do not really know at all. There's a big difference between being around these people and actually living intimately with them.

It was this immediate and personal knowledge that Paul coveted above everything else. He did not want to know Jesus simply after the flesh. He was not content with just knowing the facts about Him. He probably knew most of the facts before he became a Christian, but there were no saving qualities in external knowledge of that kind. That was man's thinking. What Paul desired was not to know Jesus as a teacher who had devout followers, but to know Him as Savior and Messiah in his own soul. It's only this knowledge of Jesus that saves even now, the knowledge that comes from having a personal experience with Him.

This is not to minimize the importance of history, but it is not through the study of the facts about Jesus that we gain the personal experience with Jesus. The Spirit must draw us to the truth. Under the tutelage of the Holy Spirit, we read the Gospel story and become keenly aware that we are not simply dealing with someone who lived and died nearly two millennia ago, but with a living person who is actually in touch with our spirit. Jesus is our God-consciousness, because through Him we know the Father.

Paul appreciated the value of other areas of knowledge. He was a scholar and a theologian. After he learned about Jesus Christ, however, they seemed to fade in importance. In Philippians, Paul is speaking as if this knowledge he desires is a future experience. But didn't Paul already know Jesus in a direct and experiential way? Yes, he did. He had known Him in that way since he met Him on the road to Damascus in Acts, chapter 9. His knowledge of the facts about Jesus changed to an experiential knowledge of Jesus Himself, but his experience was by no means confined to that great and critical occasion. It was a continuous process of discovery.

In the same way, our experiential knowledge of Jesus is always progressive. In Him, all of the treasures of knowledge and wisdom are hidden. We can say of a human friend, "I know him through and through," but no one knows Jesus Christ through and through. As Paul followed his Master throughout his life, he was forced to say:

> **Not as though I had already attained, either were already perfect: but I follow after, if that I may apprehend that for which also I am apprehended of Christ Jesus.**
>
> **Philippians 3:12**

FROM OUTER COURT TO INNER COURT

We are all taught in school that Christopher Columbus discovered America, but Columbus just landed on one of the smaller islands in the Americas. He never apprehended the vast continent before him with its tribes of peoples, great lakes, rivers, and forests. He died knowing only the barest tip of what he had discovered. So many of us have discovered a taste of God's love, but there are heights, depths, lengths, and breadths that we cannot even imagine. We should pray as Paul did for the church at Ephesus:

> **That Christ may dwell in your hearts by faith; that ye, being rooted and grounded in love,**
>
> **May be able to comprehend with all saints what is the breadth, and length, and depth, and height;**

And to know the love of Christ, which passeth knowledge, that ye might be filled with all the fulness of God.

Ephesians 3:17-19

In the Old Testament, there was an inner court to the Temple where only faithful children of Israel could go, and there was an outer court where the Gentiles could walk. In the outer court were those who knew *of* God but had no relationship with Him. Today, there are far too many outer-court worshippers who are content to live void of the intimate knowledge of Jesus. I don't mean the ungodly and the profane who are obviously strangers, but those in and out of the church who are content to know Jesus in a historical sense. They know the life of Jesus of Nazareth, but not the eternal life in Jesus Christ the Savior. They know the doctrine, but do not know Him. They know of His coming, but refuse to acknowledge His presence. They're satisfied with merely hearing about or reading about Jesus.

Paul did not say, "I *have heard of* Him in whom I believe," but "I *know* whom I have believed."

"Do you know a house on such and such a corner?"

"Yes, I know the house — it's white with a lot of glass in front."

TODAY, THERE ARE FAR TOO MANY OUTER-COURT WORSHIPPERS WHO ARE CONTENT TO LIVE VOID OF THE INTIMATE KNOWLEDGE OF JESUS.

"Well, how does the bedroom look?"

"I don't know."

"How does the kitchen look?"

"I don't know."

They know which house it is, what it looks like, and where it's located. But they don't know the essence and inner qualities of the house. Levels of knowing. How many different ways are there to know a person? I'll buy my wife something and she'll be amazed at how I knew exactly what she wanted and how thoughtful I was. I think, *After twenty years of marriage, don't you think I know you?*

Allowing God's voice to prevail over our thinking is about knowing Him in depth. The truth is, you don't get to know anyone in depth without spending a lot of time with them and going through a lot of ups and downs. To get from the outer court to the inner court of the Temple, a whole lot of things had to take place — sacrifices, purification, and entering into praise and worship. God beckons us to the Holy of Holies, to commune intimately with Him, but we must leave our flesh behind and come glorifying Him alone.

THE POWER OF HIS RESURRECTION

It was the risen Christ who appeared to Paul, and he desired to know Him and the power of His resurrection.

He wanted to know Christ in himself and himself in Christ — not a memory, not a feeling, but a power. To have the risen Christ in him, to know that He's there and what He is doing there, is to know Him and the power of His resurrection.

As we get to know Jesus intimately and develop a deeper and deeper relationship, we begin to be and act more like Him. In that sense, we begin to walk in His power.

> **He** [Jesus] **saith unto them, But whom say ye that I am?**
>
> **And Simon Peter answered and said, Thou art the Christ, the Son of the living God.**
>
> **And Jesus answered and said unto him, Blessed art thou, Simon Barjona: for flesh and blood hath not revealed it unto thee, but my Father which is in heaven.**
>
> **And I say also unto thee, That thou art Peter, and upon this rock I will build my church; and the gates of hell shall not prevail against it.**
>
> **And I will give unto thee the keys of the kingdom of heaven: and whatsoever thou shalt bind on earth shall be bound in heaven: and**

whatsoever thou shalt loose on earth shall be loosed in heaven.

Matthew 16:15-19

We have discussed keys before, and keys represent power and authority. What does Jesus mean by the keys of the kingdom? He didn't say *key* to the kingdom, He said *keys.* If you had the key to a hotel, you could get in the lobby, but not into a single room. But if you had the *keys* to the hotel, you could unlock every room in the building.

The keys to God's kingdom bring you deeper and deeper into a revelation of Him. Jesus said that His kingdom doesn't come with observation, it is *within* men. (See Luke 17:20.) The more deeply we know Him, follow His Spirit, and trust His Word, the more knowledge of Him we discover. When we walk in the intimate knowledge of Him, His power flows through our lives.

The Spirit itself beareth witness with our spirit, that we are the children of God:

And if children, then heirs; heirs of God, and joint-heirs with Christ; if so be that we suffer with him, that we may be also glorified together.

Romans 8:16-17

That the God of our Lord Jesus Christ, the Father of glory, may give unto you the

spirit of wisdom and revelation in the knowledge of him:

The eyes of your understanding being enlightened; that ye may know what is the hope of his calling, and what the riches of the glory of his inheritance in the saints,

And what is the exceeding greatness of his power to us-ward who believe, according to the working of his mighty power.

Ephesians 1:17-19

The born-again man is capable of operating on the same level of faith as Jesus. If we're born again, we are joint heirs with Jesus Christ and we have His power. If we're in Christ, we're Abraham's seed and heirs according to the promise of God's Word. (See Galatians 3:29.) What a promise!

In Genesis 24:60, the promise that the Lord made to Abraham was that his seed would possess the gate of his enemy. Then Jesus, who is Abraham's seed, gives believers His authority and power to loose things on earth that are allowed in heaven and to bind things on earth that are not allowed in heaven. This is the power God wants us to possess. What things are not allowed in heaven? There is no sickness, disease, poverty, or evil of any kind. Heaven is a healthy, happy place.

We have the power of His resurrection for use here and now. Now man's thinking is to put off our blessings until we get to heaven. "Yaaaas, brother, when we get to heaven we will have all this power and authority." But what will we do with it? There will be no demons, no battles, no evil, and no sickness. We won't need it then, but we really need it now!

I want to know Him in the power of His resurrection. Resurrection is not a matter of man's creed but of God's loving plan. It starts not from our anticipation but from real experience. Jesus Christ doesn't rise triumphantly in our creed; He rises triumphantly in our lives. Immortality is not a future gift; immortality is a present acquisition. It is good to look back and sing "Christ is risen," but the real question is, "Am I risen with Christ? Have I attained unto the resurrection that I may know Him?"

THE POWER OF HIS SUFFERINGS

Our enjoyment of the eternal benefits of Jesus Christ's suffering is dependent upon the depth of our fellowship with Him. How do we get to this level? Like Paul, I must count all these things lost. This involves sacrifice, denial of self, laying down my life for my brothers and sisters, and living in the love God has for me. I must kill my flesh in the outer court to enter into the glory of the inner court.

JESUS CHRIST DOESN'T RISE TRIUMPHANTLY IN OUR CREED; HE RISES TRIUMPHANTLY IN OUR LIVES.

I want to know Him in the fellowship of His suffering. Suffering itself, without the fellowship, does nothing. We may torture ourselves, but it does no good if we continue to live ungodly lives, without compassion for others. What we want is to suffer in the right way — in fellowship with Jesus. How did He suffer? Not by bringing suffering upon Himself or suffering for its own sake. He was the man of sorrows because His purpose was to do the will of His Father, which was to lay down His life for us.

The partnership which existed among the fishermen of Galilee and in the early Church was a fellowship in which believers had many things in common. The sign of fellowship among the true disciples of Jesus is love.

> **A new commandment I give unto you, That ye love one another; as I have loved you, that ye also love one another.**
>
> **By this shall all men know that ye are my disciples, if ye have love one to another.**
>
> **John 13:34-35**

This old commandment was: **Thou shalt not avenge, nor bear any grudge against the children of thy people, but thou shalt love thy neighbour as thyself: I am the Lord** (Leviticus 19:18). But the new commandment added something dynamic to the equation: **as I have loved you.** We can love others because Jesus loves us. We can love others the way Jesus loves us. We can lay our lives down for others as Jesus gave His life for us. We can know Him in the fellowship of His sufferings.

We must be ready at all times to lay our lives down for each other. Sacrifice. Go when we don't feel like going. Come and learn when we don't feel like learning. Love when we don't feel like loving. It is called living the crucified life.

> **And they that are Christ's have crucified the flesh with the affections and lusts.**
>
> **Galatians 5:24**

Look at this word "flesh." This word does not describe the body we wear temporarily. It refers to the evil, the sin, and the corruption that goes with the body. It was a common philosophical term used to summarize all that was low, unspiritual, and against God.

Crucifying the flesh is not living a miserable life. We do not escape from the power of the world and the flesh by shutting ourselves off from everything and denying ourselves any pleasure in life. No, we simply must serve God, and others as He directs us, instead of ourselves.

Man's greatest enemy is himself, not the devil. In the Garden of Eden, the Tree of Life was a means by which man could live forever with God, and the Tree of the

Knowledge of Good and Evil was a means by which man could live independently from God. God put these two trees in the Garden to test the heart of man, to see whom he would serve — himself or God.

Rather than choosing the Tree of Life, man chose the Tree of the Knowledge of Good and Evil. He would rather develop his life as he saw fit and do his own thing. Today, we have a choice between the Tree of Life, which is the cross of Jesus Christ, and the Tree of the Knowledge of Good and Evil, which is our carnal mind. We will always have to make a choice between the two.

We feel something is supposed to happen to our self-nature when we get saved, but nothing happens. In fact, sometimes there is no improvement. Jesus didn't come to improve self, but to replace it with Himself. He came to take out the stony heart of self. We can't discipline it. There's no good self or bad self as far as God is concerned. To be made conformable unto His death we must kill self.

The Christian is of no use to God until he dies to self. He cannot live completely for God as long as he continues to live in self. So when we say we need to crucify the flesh, we are not referring to killing our physical body. God wants us to see what Jesus' death was all about: He gave no place to self; but simply served His Father.

Because Jesus died for us, we should die to sin. And because He died for us, we should live for Him.

> **I am crucified with Christ: nevertheless I live; yet not I, but Christ liveth in me: and the life which I now live in the flesh I live by the faith of the Son of God, who loved me, and who gave himself for me.**
>
> **Galatians 2:20**

> **And he said to them all, If any man will come after me, let him deny himself, and take up his cross daily, and follow me.**
>
> **Luke 9:23**

To know Jesus in the fellowship of His sufferings, to know Him in the power of His resurrection, and to stay in God's order, we must die to our old ways of thinking and allow God's voice to lead us. Then He will give us the keys to the kingdom, and we will receive power from on high. With that power, not only will our own lives be transformed, but we can change the world.

Conclusion: INTO THE WORLD

As more and more members of the body of Christ learn how to break out of man's thinking and get into God's order, the fire of God's grace will spread. It will hit every city and transform the earth. If you don't have a fire, kindle the fire!

The fire of divine grace, kindled by God's Word in our spirits, comes like light to the intellect and illuminates. It comes like heat to the heart and inflames. It comes like strength to the will and energizes it. We must keep it burning!

How do we maintain it? It's one thing to build a fire. It's another thing to keep it ablaze! The fire on the altar of Israel, kindled from heaven, had to be kept burning by natural and human resources. The priest had to go to the altar every day to take away the ashes. The ashes represent our sins, the things we know are wrong and lie heavy upon our consciences. To maintain God's order in our lives, we can't allow sins to build up and smother the fire.

Then the priest had to feed the fire with the right fuel. Feed the fire of grace with God's Word. Pray in the Spirit. Crucify your self and live your life in Him and for Him. I had a breakdown, so I would be bold enough to break up so I could break out. I died to self and God raised me up because I was willing to give up all for Him. I'm dead to self, but alive in Jesus in the power of His resurrection. I am knowing Him in the power of His resurrection and the fellowship of His sufferings. I thank Him for letting me share in being made conformable unto His death. It has made me stronger in Him.

The death of Jesus was real, but not permanent. He got down, but He got up and He got out. My breakdown was real, but not permanent. I got down, but I got up and I got out. Although the devil had me confused, I kept my mind, because God will keep you in perfect peace if you keep your mind stayed on Him. I was safe because I asked Him to keep my mind. If *I* would have kept my mind, I wouldn't have one today!

Today I know who I am. I'm confident. I'm ready, I'm prepared. Yet, all of these attitudes have their source in Jesus now, not in myself or my abilities and gifts. Whatever it takes, I choose to be one who lives in the fresh newness of life, one of those who are alive from the dead. Nothing else matters; nothing else is important.

WHATEVER IT TAKES, I CHOOSE TO BE ONE WHO LIVES IN THE FRESH NEWNESS OF LIFE, ONE OF THOSE WHO ARE ALIVE FROM THE DEAD. NOTHING ELSE MATTERS; NOTHING ELSE IS IMPORTANT.

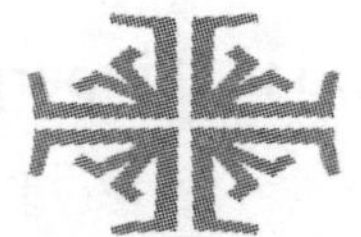

When the fire of God's grace burns in you and you get into God's order, you'll never be the same. When I broke out, the fire of God consumed me and I'll never be the same again. My life and ministry are totally transformed. The anointing God has placed on me scares the devil because he knows it's the anointing that destroys the yoke. (See Isaiah 10:27.)

My purpose now is to do God's will through the power of His resurrection. I have resurrection power in my spirit, soul, and body. There is no fear. The Bible tells us in 2 Timothy 1:7 that God has not given us the spirit of fear but of power, love, and a sound mind. And that power is not just to feel good and sit around and watch television!

That power — the resurrection power of the Holy Ghost — is to preach, teach, lay hands on the sick, cast out demons, and set the captives free. I did not write this book to talk about myself, get something off my chest, draw attention to myself, or make some extra money. I wrote this book to set captives free.

That fire I talked about earlier is the all-consuming fire of God to save the lost and make disciples, to bring His children home and love them, heal them, and restore them. We are each called to this purpose, and as we fulfill this call, we will discover the heart of our Father — the greatest treasure and reward of all.

EPILOGUE:

FROM OUTSIDE IN

BY BISHOP CLARENCE E. MCCLENDON

John, the beloved apostle and writer, began the epistle known in the canon of Scripture as 1 John with the words, **That which...we have heard, which we have seen with our eyes, which we looked upon, and our hands have handled....** He did so to establish, in essence, that that which he was about to articulate was neither hearsay nor secondhand information, but the report of an eyewitness.

Upon receiving the request from the International Presiding Bishop of the Full Gospel Baptist Church Fellowship, our Beloved Bishop and my friend, Bishop Paul S. Morton Sr., to contribute to this book, recounting his experience and recovery from the attack of the enemy, I was pleased to be asked to give what is an eyewitness account to the strength and providence of our Lord Jesus and the power of the Holy Spirit over all the works of the devil; to hush the mouth of the gainsayer and the innocently misinformed regarding this series of events.

First of all, let me say that it is the height of naiveté to believe that we will be allowed to apprehend, possess, and walk in "book of Acts power" and not also be the target of "book of Acts persecution." If we desire to walk in the power which we observe in the lives of the apostles, we must also be prepared to handle (and properly discern) the attacks which we observe in their lives, for these too are "written for our instruction."

I had the privilege of being in telephone communication with our beloved Bishop during the series of events which not only weighed heavily upon him, but to my perception, also triggered the attack upon him. During discussion and prayer, our beloved Bishop exhibited both soundness of mind and the contagious optimism that those of us who know him well have come to expect. He articulated at that time that he was in need of rest, but had some appointments he needed to fulfill, and that our Lord had been dealing strongly with him about some significant issues. I had already been informed that the Bishop's heavy ministry schedule, administrative concerns, and the "care of all the churches," which constantly rested upon him, were taking their toll. Moreover, I learned that some of the people closest to him in the day-to-day operations were in ardent prayer and very concerned. To the natural eye and ear, all was well or would soon be, but we have been given the Holy Spirit so that we should not depend on the natural eyes or ears, but be able to discern what "eyes cannot see, and ears cannot hear."

My discernment told me that our beloved Bishop needed prayer, and the Holy Spirit informed me that I was to make a trip to New Orleans as soon as possible. I immediately called our church in Los Angeles to prayer and converted one of our Wednesday night services to a season of prayer for our beloved Bishop. I then made plans to make the trip to New Orleans.

Let me say that it was very obvious to me before my arrival in New Orleans, in direct contact with the Bishop, that he had been *very strongly dealt with* by the Spirit of God and had received revelation and instruction which he at that time was not at liberty to share. It is important to note this, because I believe it is *key* to the attack upon him.

On the day of my arrival in New Orleans, I was taken immediately from the airport to the Bishop's presence. Along with a few others, I proceeded to spend the next fourteen hours in conversation, intercession, praise, and natural assistance with Bishop and his family. I was present and assisted in his initial admittance for medical attention in New Orleans. I thoroughly agreed with the decision to ascertain medical analysis and attention for the Bishop. I believe that medicine is one of God's healing streams for man's wholeness.

I knew, however, that we were not merely dealing with a physical, mental, or emotional challenge, but a spiritual attack, and that spiritual discernment and warfare would be necessary. I also knew that *spiritual discernment* would have to precede *spiritual warfare.* It is so important as we deal in the spiritual realm that we discern by the Spirit the situations before us so that, as the apostle Paul says, we run "not with uncertainty" and "fight not as those who beat the air." (See 1 Corinthians 9:26.)

Being not a novice in dealing with spiritual matters, and having some knowledge of the grace of God given to me, I recognized that a part of my assignment for being present at the time was to assist in discerning the matters at hand for the purpose of prayer. When I first encountered our beloved Bishop at his home in New Orleans, I set myself to listen to the voice of the Spirit. I was not sure that Bishop recognized me. I believe he did, but I was not certain. One thing was certain. The spirit of the man was strong. Although under obvious mental duress and physical exhaustion, he was praying in the Spirit, quoting Scripture, and during a glorious outbreak of a visitation, we prayed in the Spirit, sang praises to God, and did

It is so important as we deal in the spiritual realm that we discern by the Spirit the situations before us so that, as the apostle Paul says, we run "not with uncertainty" and "fight not as those who beat the air." (See 1 Corinthians 9:26.)

warfare with the Word of God against the attack of the devil for almost an hour. I cannot overemphasize the glory of the outbreak of the visitation — the very presence of God filled the room!

Seldom had I been in a situation where the three parts of man (spirit, soul, and body) were so obviously distinct, and where the obvious power of a spiritual man filled with the Holy Spirit was so clearly displayed as being in control. It was as if despite the attack or signals the mind, will, and emotions (soulish ream) were receiving, and in spite of the physical trauma the body was under, the spirit of Bishop Morton, indwelt by the Holy Spirit, was warring and refusing to yield to the attack. It was powerful, to say the least.

The spirit of man is the candle of the Lord (Proverbs 20:27). It is our spirit that the Spirit of God lights, illuminates, and fills! **The word of God is quick, and powerful, and sharper than any twoedged sword, piercing even to the dividing asunder of soul and spirit** (Hebrews 4:12). The Word of God in the spirit of man gives man's spirit dominion over the activity of his soul *by that living Word!*

This was no demonic possession. I do not believe that the spirit of a man indwelt by the Holy Spirit (which our Bishop certainly is) can be possessed. Let us never make such an error! The Scripture leaves no room for such a thought. It is possible, however, through traumatic events, exhaustion, or a variety of other situations, for the enemy to gain access to the mind of even the Spirit-filled believer and *oppress* (not possess) the *mind* (not the spirit) of the individual. To the one unskillful in the Word or undiscerning in the Spirit, these two can often appear very similar, especially where one is dealing with "higher" spirits of darkness attacking a general in the faith.

In an attempt to avoid exhausting every aspect of my involvement in these events, and resisting any temptation to sound like the authority on the matters at hand, let me finish my contribution with an *observation*, a *revelation* that I received by the Spirit while present with our beloved Bishop, and a brief *exhortation* to the believers, especially those of the Full Gospel Baptist Church Fellowship.

First, I know from experience that one of the challenges all men of vision have is attempting to balance the spiritual work we must do with the natural limitations of time and space. I often wish I had a glorified body to do this glorious work. But the fact of the matter is, we **have this treasure in earthen vessels** (2 Corinthians 4:7). The burden of responsibility that men are given can often seem overwhelming, and it is certain that we are given grace beyond others to fulfill that responsibility. On the other hand, if we do not *rest*, and have regular seasons to **come ye yourselves apart into a desert place, and**

rest a while (Mark 6:31) as Jesus instructed His disciples, we are not only in danger of burning out, but of getting out of order, which is the more significant point.

If we constantly violate and override the promptings of the Spirit or the signals of our physical bodies, we will open a door and give place to the devil, enabling him to subject us to attacks that we might otherwise be able to avoid. (I also speak to myself!) I believe that the weight of spiritual and administrative responsibility, coupled with the intense zeal and burden of ministry, could have been contributing factors to what befell our beloved Bishop.

I shall never forget, while reading the account of Jesus being awakened from sleep by the disciples and still possessing the power to rebuke the winds and waves and have them obey, that the Holy Spirit spoke to my heart, saying, "You can be just as anointed rising from sleep as rising from prayer if it's what I have called for!"

Secondly, it was while sitting privately and personally with Bishop Morton that the Spirit of God said to me in the midst of my visit to New Orleans that He had visited the Bishop in a profound way and had given him instruction, insight, and revelation, which he was not at liberty to share at that time. In addition, we must believe that we are living in the last days, that the glory of the latter house is to be greater than the glory of the former house, that the

Spirit of God is still dealing with the hearts of men today, giving revelation and insight, and that living apostles (as our Bishop is) are still among us, all a part of the Full Gospel! Then, we must also believe that according to **the abundance of the revelations, there was given to me a thorn in the flesh, a messenger of Satan to buffet me....**

If we are living in the days of God's power, then Satan's devices are still the same, and he is still sending messengers to attempt to thwart men who are receiving revelation from the Spirit for their generation. This is not to equate our Bishop with the apostle Paul of old, but it is the revelation, not the man, that the attack was sent against. We cannot think we can change a generation and not meet head-on with the satanic guardians of the generation we are called to change!

Finally, I must discuss the exhortation. Acts 12 records the account of Herod being moved upon by the spirit of the age. After having slain the apostle James, and seeing that it pleased the Jews, he decided to take another apostle and slay him also. Peter was therefore taken and chained, awaiting execution.

In Acts12:5-6 NIV it says, **So Peter was kept in prison, but the *church was earnestly praying to God for him.* The night before Herod was to bring him to trial, *Peter was sleeping....*** We all know of Peter's miraculous,

WE CANNOT THINK WE CAN CHANGE A GENERATION AND NOT MEET HEAD-ON WITH THE SATANIC GUARDIANS OF THE GENERATION WE ARE CALLED TO CHANGE!

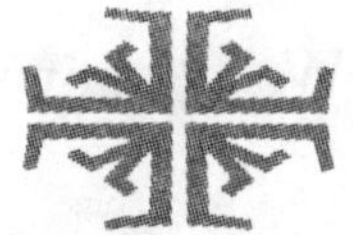

angelic deliverance from that prison. Although chains fell off supernaturally and iron gates opened on their own, we often miss the importance of this story.

The apostle Peter's deliverance here was not the product of his own prayers and intercession. He was asleep! It was as if the people of the church determined, "Devil, we will not let you take another apostle from us! You took James while we were asleep, now we're awake and praying and the apostles can sleep without fear!" Church, our apostles need to be able to rest knowing that prayers are constantly surrounding them. And Church, we need to know and believe that *our* prayers for the men of God avail much!

We thank God for the glorious deliverance of Bishop Paul S. Morton Sr. from the attack of the enemy. Let us never cease to pray for him. Let us seize the call to prayer for him and all men of God as together we seek to "Change a Generation."

ABOUT THE AUTHOR

Bishop Paul Sylvester Morton was born in Windsor, Ontario, Canada on July 30, 1950. He is the son of the late Bishop C. L. Morton and the late Evangelist Matilda E. Morton. It was prophesied before his birth that he would carry the mantle of his father and preach the Gospel with a special anointing. Growing up, he also exemplified a special talent in music, but God called him to preach the Gospel in 1967. In 1972, he moved to New Orleans, Louisiana.

A man of great vision, Bishop Morton began humbly in New Orleans, Louisiana. He was devoted to the ministry and later accepted the position of associate pastor at Greater St. Stephen Missionary Baptist Church, under the pastorate of Reverend Percy Simpson. He also attended and graduated from the Union Baptist Seminary of Louisiana.

In 1974, the Greater St. Stephen family experienced the tragic, accidental death of Pastor Simpson and Paul S. Morton was installed pastor in January 1975. Under his leadership, the spiritual, financial, and numerical growth has been phenomenal. In 1980 the church moved from a 600-seat sanctuary to a 2000-seat sanctuary built adjacent to the original edifice.

Shortly after his appointment, Bishop Morton fell in love with the woman whom he says, “makes my life complete.” Elder Debra Brown Morton, a daughter of Greater St. Stephen, became his wife in December of 1976. They have three children: Jasmine, Paul Jr., and Christiann. Although tender in years, they are busy in the ministry with their parents.

In 1985, after averaging 33 revivals a year, God instructed Bishop Morton to initiate a Pastoral Bible Class. Then in 1986, he instituted a weekly Deliverance Service, fulfilling the Word of God by laying hands on the sick and praying for the needs of God’s people. In 1988, Greater St. Stephen East was added to Bishop Morton’s oversight. This satellite church built an auditorium in 1992, and in 1997, the Lord led Bishop Morton to the Westbank area of New Orleans.

Bishop Morton now officiates seven services on Sunday to his over 20,000-member Greater St. Stephen Full Gospel Baptist Church congregation. Then he does two weekly Bible “Word Explosions.”

Bishop Morton has a successful daily television program and radio broadcast called, "Changing a Generation," which are aired in several areas nationwide. He has written many books, several handbooks, and has recorded five albums with the Greater St. Stephen Mass Choir. He has also done a nationally recognized solo album and has been featured on other well-known Gospel recording artists' albums.

On March 19, 1993, Pastor Paul Morton was consecrated Bishop. He then founded the Full Gospel Baptist Church Fellowship, over whom he serves as Presiding Bishop. More than 30,000 people attended the first conference in 1994 and it continues to grow every year.

Bishop Paul Morton's commitment to his community is evident by his participation on the Board of One Church One Addict. He is also the President of the Paul S. Morton Sr. Scholarship Foundation and the President of the Greater St. Stephen Full Gospel Baptist School of Ministry. He is an Honorary Councilman and has laid hands on and prayed for the Mayor, the Governor, the National Black Caucus, Congress, and the President of the United States. He lives his life according to Isaiah 1:17, **Learn to do well; seek judgment, relieve the oppressed, judge the fatherless, plead for the widow.**

To contact Bishop Morton, write:

Bishop Paul S. Morton

Greater St. Stephen Full Gospel Baptist Church

9661 Lake Forest Boulevard

New Orleans, Louisiana 70127

or call:

(504) 244-6800

Additional copies of this book and other book titles
from **Albury Publishing** are
available at your local bookstore.

Albury Publishing
Tulsa, Oklahoma

For a complete list of our titles,
visit us at our web site:
www.alburypublishing.com

For international and Canadian orders,
please contact:

Access Sales International
2448 East 81st Street
Suite 4900
Tulsa, Oklahoma 74137
Phone 918-523-5590 Fax 918-496-2822